MAKING LIFE EASY

A SIMPLE GUIDE TO A DIVINELY INSPIRED LIFE

ALSO BY CHRISTIANE NORTHRUP, M.D.

Books

Goddesses Never Age

Mother-Daughter Wisdom

The Secret Pleasures of Menopause

The Wisdom of Menopause

The Wisdom of Menopause Journal

Women's Bodies, Women's Wisdom

The Secret Pleasures of Menopause Playbook

Beautiful Girl

Audio/Video Programs

Goddesses Never Age

Creating Health

The Empowering Women Gift Collection
(with Louise L. Hay, Susan Jeffers, Ph.D.,
and Caroline Myss, Ph.D.)

Menopause and Beyond

Mother-Daughter Wisdom

The Power of Joy

The Secret Pleasures of Menopause

Women's Bodies, Women's Wisdom

Inside-Out Wellness
(with Dr. Wayne W. Dyer)

Miscellaneous

Women's Bodies, Women's Wisdom Oracle Cards

MAKING LIFE EASY

A SIMPLE GUIDE TO A DIVINELY INSPIRED LIFE

CHRISTIANE NORTHRUP, M.D.

HAY HOUSE, INC.
Carlsbad, California • New York City
London • Sydney • Johannesburg
Vancouver • New Delhi

Published and distributed in the United States by: Hay House, Inc.: www .hayhouse.com® • *Published and distributed in Australia by:* Hay House Australia Pty. Ltd.: www.hayhouse.com.au • *Published and distributed in the United Kingdom by:* Hay House UK, Ltd.: www.hayhouse.co.uk • *Published and distributed in the Republic of South Africa by:* Hay House SA (Pty), Ltd.: www.hayhouse.co.za • *Distributed in Canada by:* Raincoast Books: www .raincoast.com • *Published in India by:* Hay House Publishers India: www .hayhouse.co.in

Cover design: Tricia Breidenthal • *Interior design:* Pamela Homan
Indexer: Laura Ogar

Library of Congress Cataloging-in-Publication Data

Names: Northrup, Christiane, author.
Title: Making life easy : a simple guide to a divinely inspired life /
    Christiane Northrup, M.D.
Description: 1st edition. | Carlsbad, California : Hay House, Inc., [2016] |
    Includes bibliographical references and index.
Identifiers: LCCN 2016028317 | ISBN 9781401951467 (hardcover : alk. paper)
Subjects: LCSH: Spirituality. | Spiritual life.
Classification: LCC BL624 .N676 2016 | DDC 204/.4--dc23 LC record available at
https://lccn.loc.gov/2016028317

Hardcover ISBN: 978-1-4019-5146-7

10 9 8 7 6 5 4 3 2 1
1st edition, December 2016

Printed in the United States of America

*For all who have the courage
to think for themselves and
live from the truth
they feel in their hearts*

CONTENTS

INTRODUCTION

If you've read any of my other books or followed my work, you probably think of me as a Western-trained ob/gyn physician and surgeon who has been offering women effective alternatives to drugs and surgery for decades. I've been working to help people think about their health and their bodies in a more empowered way. What you may not know is that from the time I was a teenager I've been enthralled with all things spiritual and metaphysical—the forces that cannot be seen but that influence us profoundly. Though conversations about angels, reincarnation, and Spirit guides are not standard in the hospitals and clinics where I've spent decades, I have come to the conclusion that life without spiritual understanding, especially when you're faced with pain or loss, is very difficult. Unless we understand that there is a much bigger picture that requires faith, we are too often left feeling like powerless victims of forces beyond our control. We slowly start to believe that "Life's a bitch and then you die."

But life doesn't have to be like this. It doesn't have to be nearly as hard as most of us make it. All it takes is a shift of perspective, a move to taking the bigger view. I've known this for years—lifetimes, in fact—and the time has finally come for me to share what I've always known about how to make your life easy. That's what this book is about.

The essence of everything you will learn in these pages comes down to this: To live an easy life, you have to align with the Divine part of yourself. In fact, you have to let it lead your life. This is not the same as waiting for some kind of Divine force outside of you to come swooping in to rescue you from your life. That's not how it works. You have to make an effort to make changes. But when you align your personal will with Divine will, then you can move mountains.

Much of what I'm going to teach you in this book is not logical, so chances are good that your logical left brain will find this information challenging. That part of you will always want scientific proof. But life doesn't work that way. We're here to develop faith—faith in things that our five senses can't see, touch, hear, or feel, and that our intellects can't prove. We've all been trained to believe that randomized double-blind controlled studies will keep us safe and tell us what to do. But clinging to logical, rational linear thinking is what keeps life hard. Waiting for some authority other than our Divine connection to tell us what to do keeps us stuck in victimhood and pain.

Think of this book as an owner's manual for bringing heaven down to earth. When you learn to align with your Divine self, your life becomes easier. You have access to guidance that will take you in the right direction. You're able to make choices that are in your best interest. Things will simply flow, and you'll be happy and filled with peace.

My journey with the Divine began years ago. When I was about 12 years old, I was babysitting for some family friends when I spied a small box that had come in the mail. The words *Natives of Eternity* were written on the box, which had come from a place called the Christward Ministry. Intrigued—actually beyond intrigued—I felt compelled to open the box. I knew it was wrong, but I was overcome by the need to know more.

Inside the box I found a book called *Natives of Eternity*, which was written by Christian mystic Flower Newhouse. It was all about angels. And nature spirits. And devas of the wind, water, and air. There were descriptions and paintings of all the beings who oversaw the plants, the wind, birth, death, and even music.

Something in me leapt to attention. This book confirmed everything that I was born knowing. It told me I was right to believe that there's much more to life than what we can see with our eyes and hear with our ears. It told me the kingdom of heaven is all around us, ready and waiting to assist us with life on earth. Every page was amazing. I couldn't stop reading.

When I got home, I told my mother all about the book—and that I had opened the box. Distressed by my transgression but happy about my excitement, she called Gretchen, who had hired me to babysit. She called to apologize but also to find out more about the book. Soon enough, I had my very own copy—a gift from Gretchen, who also gave me another gift. She suggested that we meet for brunch to talk about what I'd learned from the book. She had been to the Christward Ministry in California many times, and she knew Reverend Newhouse. Thus began a series of meetings with Gretchen during which we would spend our time delighting in discussions of angels, nature Spirits, and the wonders of life.

As our meetings progressed, I got even more interested in the realm of what we cannot see. I started reading anything I could find that was related to this. I learned about reincarnation and how our current struggles have actually been carried over from past lives as lessons, not as punishment for being "bad." Instead they are meant to further the evolution of our Souls by bringing light into darkness.

I also learned about the true nature of self—how our identities are made up of our egos, our Spirits, and our Souls. We are Souls in bodies, but our connection with the Divine is always there, always available to guide us.

I learned about the power of the mind to change our bodies and our lives. Our thoughts manifest in physical outcomes. We have the power to bring Spirit into matter.

My meetings with Gretchen and my exploration of the unseen continued until I went to medical school. Everything I learned in that time solidified within me a deep and abiding knowledge that there is more to life than we have been led to believe and that our bodies, minds, and Spirits are truly connected. No part of us can be completely healthy unless every part of us is.

When I went to medical school, however, my confidence in this innate knowledge was not something I could talk about openly. Nor did I trust it completely. Yes, deep down I still knew it to be true, but it's hard to keep these principles at the top of your mind when they go against everything you're experiencing on a day-to-day basis.

Standard Western medicine is based on obsolete thinking—the old Newtonian cause-and-effect model. You are exposed to a germ, you get sick. It's a formula. There is no magic in it. Modern medicine uses statistics and large populations to create these formulas, and it treats us all according to demographics and the "herd mentality." If you're 50, you need a colonoscopy because that's when your colon starts to break down. The belief is that your body is a machine that is not connected to your thoughts, your emotions, or your Spirit. If you take good care of it, it should work—until it doesn't. Because, like all machines, it will wear out. And there is absolutely nothing you can do about it.

So this is the idea that was being preached to me throughout medical school, throughout my residency, throughout the beginning of my career. While I felt that this couldn't be true, it's hard to argue against it when you're exhausted and frazzled from working and studying nonstop.

But as time wore on, I could no longer ignore the calls coming from deep down inside me. I couldn't, in good conscience, just cover up symptoms with drugs or surgical procedures. I had to do better for my patients. I had to get back to what I had known when I began: No part of us can be completely healthy unless every part of us is. The Spirit, the mind, and the body cannot be separated.

So if you want good health in your physical body, you also need to look to the health of your emotional and spiritual bodies. When you do this, every part of your life will simply start to flow, smoothly and easily. That's what this book is about: making life easy.

In these pages, you'll see just how the Spirit, the mind, and the body are connected and how caring for one means you are caring for the others. With simple exercises and practical advice, I'll teach you how to bolster your physical health not by simply eating well and moving regularly—though these are a part of it—but also by listening to the voice of your Soul and tapping into Divine guidance.

You truly do have the power to make your life easy on all levels. So often, the key to creating your own personal heaven on earth is deliberately and consciously letting your Spirit take the lead. If you do that, you will know just how to create the life you want. If, on the other hand, you believe that you have no power, that your problems are caused by bad luck, bad genes, or the wrong family, then there truly isn't much that will work out very well for you over the long haul.

The work of this book is simple and easy. The only challenge comes from the fact that your ego wants to be in charge instead of learning to be of service to your Divine self. But that's what this book will teach you. It takes a little discipline and focus, but, believe me, you can't even imagine how beautiful it can be.

CHAPTER 1

You Are a Divine Being Temporarily Living in a Human Body

The human body is the best picture of the human soul.

— LUDWIG WITTGENSTEIN

When I was a teenager, I read every book I could find on Edgar Cayce. Cayce, who we would now call a medical intuitive, was known as the Sleeping Prophet because he'd go into a hypnotic trance and then, knowing only a person's name and address, diagnose their medical condition and suggest the right treatment—and this was almost always after everything else had failed. Born on a farm in Kentucky in 1877, Cayce had no knowledge of medicine or anatomy, making him an unlikely candidate for providing medical advice. He had only a grammar-school education, had read only the Bible, and worked as a photographer. But when he was 24 years old, he lost his voice. He tried everything to recover, and as a last resort he turned to hypnosis, which was becoming popular at the time. While he was under, Cayce successfully described the condition of his own vocal cords and what to do about his problem, and when he awoke, his speaking voice had been restored. Both Cayce and his family were astounded. Word

1

spread, and soon he was using his diagnostic and curative powers to help thousands of people recover their health.

In 1923 Cayce moved from simply giving medical advice to answering much bigger questions such as "What is the meaning of life?" "What is the true nature of humans?" and "Why are we here?" The answers that came forth were based on several thousand "life readings"—information on people's past lives. When asked more about where he was getting his information, he gave two sources. One was the unconscious or subconscious mind of whomever he was reading at the time. The other was what Carl Jung called the Collective Unconscious, or the Akashic Records. Cayce's ponderings on life and health led him to a powerful conclusion about physical health:

The Spirit is Life

The Mind is the Builder

The Physical is the Result

This quote struck a deep chord of truth within me, and that truth has guided me for my entire life—all through medical school, residency, my years of medical practice, and beyond. I entered medical school knowing that illnesses don't just jump out of the closet and land on us. There are much bigger forces at work. Divine forces. Knowing this has made *all* the difference in how I have treated people who have come to me with health concerns and how I live my own life. Without acknowledging these bigger forces—forces that our intellects can't wrap themselves around—life on planet Earth can easily turn into a miserable hell of constant worry about our health. Not to mention a constant battle to get our bodies to "behave." A hell in which we're led to believe that we can't trust our bodies, that we are universally vulnerable to everything that is "going around," and that our bodies require constant monitoring—and prescription drugs—in order to stay healthy. Catching disease early, or getting a vaccine, is our only chance. And death is always a failure.

This fear-based mind-set can also lead to great doubt and frustration in other parts of our lives. Not acknowledging the power of the Divine can keep us stranded in painful situations that go against everything we believe in. We can get stuck in jobs we hate. With relationships that detract from our lives rather than add to them. With a simple feeling of being lost, uncertain of what decisions to make.

But there's another way. A much better way. When we acknowledge the Divine part of ourselves—God coming through us *as* us—the whole ball game changes. Life just works. If we align and co-create with the Divine—our Souls and our Spirits—life becomes a grand and exciting adventure of consciously bringing Spirit into matter and reveling in our physical bodies while knowing that we aren't our bodies. We are no longer ignorant victims of our circumstances. We are powerful players in the game of life! We can create lives that are full, and happy, and healthy, and joyous, and radiant. We can be fully human and embodied while also knowing in our bone marrow that we are immortal, unlimited beings.

So what does this look like in our lives? What do I mean by "life just works"? Well, it means that we live robustly in all aspects of life—physically, emotionally, and spiritually.

On a physical and emotional level, when we live from this perspective, we know that painful physical symptoms and emotions are signals from our Souls. They are trying to get our attention, asking us to turn inward and see what's really happening. These are the keys to living fuller, more meaningful lives—not "punishment" for not doing something right in the past!

On the spiritual plane, when life just works, you make decisions that are good for you both mentally and physically. You are tapped into your true essence, which allows you to follow your passions and spread love and light to every person and circumstance you encounter. Your work, your friendships, your activities—everything works to bring you up to a higher level so you can lead an extraordinary life.

When life just works, you live longer. Your body and mind work better. You experience health and happiness. You are able to see what's truly important so you can live in a way that creates no regrets.

Fear to Faith: The Key to Making Life Easy

The unity of body, mind, and Spirit has long been ignored in our quest for a good life. When searching for physical health, we turn to Western medicine, which operates from a reductionistic and obsolete model that treats symptoms as inconvenient things to be managed by masking them with drugs or sometimes surgery. You can see this in the frightening statistics about prescription drug use in the United States. Mayo Clinic researchers have found that 70 percent of all Americans are on at least one prescription drug—and many are on more than one. The most commonly prescribed are antibiotics, opioid painkillers, and antidepressants. The belief system of "better living through chemistry" runs so deep that when people like my mother, age 90, or my doctor friend Gladys, age 95, go to a doctor, the staff can't believe they're prescription free! They are certain there must be a mistake. When the majority of the population is medicated, it's clear that something is dreadfully wrong. Medicating symptoms on an ongoing basis is a lot like putting duct tape over the indicator lights on the dashboard of your car—instead of looking under the hood to see what your engine is telling you it requires.

When we can acknowledge that our thoughts, beliefs, and circumstances and the agenda of our Souls all affect our physical and mental health dramatically, we start to see the power of each of the pieces of the puzzle described by Edgar Cayce: Spirit, mind, and body. If we align with the immense power of the Divine we, quite literally, have the keys to our own kingdom.

To fully understand the relationship between body, mind, and Spirit is to see that there is actually no separation between these parts. They all influence one another, and to focus on improving one brings better health and well-being to the others. We cannot simply look at physical health. Or mental health. Or spiritual health. We must look at them all together. We must bring each of these up to its highest state in order to live a full, healthy, happy life.

The Spirit Is Life

Let's begin by looking at the first piece of Cayce's philosophy: *The Spirit is Life*. To me, this refers to both the Soul and the Spirit. While these two terms are often used interchangeably, they are actually very different aspects of the Divine; however, they are both part of the Divine that makes up who you are. Your physical body is just a small part of the vastness of who you really are—like a drop of water in the ocean. Our bodies contain our Souls, which are connected to our Spirits. Our Spirits—or what some call our inner beings or higher selves—live outside of this material realm. Tapping into the Divine is tapping into the highest part of ourselves. We are all part of God. And you get to call the Divine anything you want: your Higher Power, Buddha, God, Jesus, Allah, the Goddess, Great Spirit—you name it. It's all your choice. There is no one "right" answer here. But no matter what you call it, to access the Divine part of yourself, you have to raise your vibration and begin the process of remembering this and communicating directly. Don't make this too complicated. Just know that you are part of God.

I think of the Spirit as the enlightened "always in the light" part of us—the nonphysical part of ourselves that is not actually in our bodies but instead vibrating at a higher rate. The Spirit part of us is all-knowing and all-seeing. It is crucial that we know this part of ourselves. Our Spirits look on and remain above the fray—offering insights along the way, but not participating in the pain and suffering that are so often part of being in a body.

Soul, on the other hand, is embodied. It is down and in. The Soul brings us into our bodies, and our bodies are where the Soul work gets done. The Soul speaks to us through our bodies. And its lessons come through our bodies in many ways, including pain and illness. These

5

experiences are not punishment for being bad. They are Soul-making opportunities. Soul is the intermediary between Spirit and ego.

The ego is responsible for our personal will—the part of us that must be developed enough to get up every morning and go to school and do homework or get up off the chair and exercise. Without personal will, absolutely nothing of value ever gets accomplished. And while there is no doubt that our personal will must be developed, we must be careful in how we do this. The development of individual will is often a big part of why we took birth in the first place. However, our personal will must be aligned with Divine will—the agenda our Souls picked before birth.

To align the Spirit, Soul, and ego is one key to creating a life that works. If you know how to properly work with your Soul and your Spirit on the earthly plane, you will be able to control the thoughts and emotions that can put you in either your own personal heaven or your own personal hell.

The Mind Is the Builder

"All impulses of thought have a tendency to clothe themselves in their physical equivalent." This quote comes from Napoleon Hill, who wrote the classic book *Think and Grow Rich,* which was published back in 1937. And it explains exactly what Cayce was talking about when he said, "The mind is the builder": Thoughts held over time greatly affect all areas of our lives. The quality of the thoughts we think creates the quality of the lives we live.

Everyone understands that thoughts and emotions can put us in a miserable mental state, but we have learned that they also affect the health of the body. Every thought we think is accompanied by an emotion—each of which has a distinct biochemistry associated with it. Thoughts of empowerment, love, and support feel good and result in an increase in immunity and a decrease in stress hormones that create wear and tear on the physical body. Thoughts of revenge, sadness, or anger feel bad. And held over time, they are associated with chemicals in the body that cause cellular inflammation—the root cause of most degenerative disease. Pretty simple, right?

But it goes even deeper than simply the hormonal influence on our current physical body. A thought that is repeated over and over again becomes a belief. And beliefs held over time actually become our biology. Our beliefs have the power to affect our genetic expression. Biological and neurochemical changes in our bodies associated with these beliefs determine which genes get expressed and which remain dormant. Hence we have more control over our biology than we've been led to believe.

The connection between our thoughts, our emotions, our beliefs, and our biology has now been thoroughly documented by many, including Dr. Bruce Lipton in his book *The Biology of Belief* and Dr. Mario Martinez in his book *The MindBody Code*—a book in which he also describes the devastating biologic effects of shame, abandonment, and betrayal.

The bottom line is this: When it comes to thoughts, we always have the choice to choose the thought that feels better. This becomes much easier when we're aligned with our Spirits and our Souls. When you choose thoughts that are aligned with your true nature instead of based in fear, you are always going with the most empowering option. And given the connection between our thoughts, emotions, and biology, developing this skill is crucial.

The Physical Is the Result

The body is created by our beliefs and thoughts—whether they are aligned with Spirit or not. But concentrating on your thoughts is not nearly enough to create a physical body that makes life easy. It's not enough to have a spiritual practice or even know about your Soul and your Spirit. To truly flourish, you have to pay attention to your body, taking care of it and meeting its needs. No matter how much you pray or meditate, you still need to eat. And to create the best body to make life easy, you need to know how to move, rest, and hydrate. Simple practices of movement and eating the right foods help preserve the quality of your tissues and your brain.

Just like each of the other aspects of making life easy, the body is intimately connected to the vitality of more than just itself. It is quite literally connected to and fueled by the same source that created the universe.

Working with Body, Mind, and Spirit

For years I have been fascinated by near-death experiences and the reports about heaven that come from these. I've also been astounded by miraculous physical recoveries that have followed near-death experiences and illnesses that should have been fatal. These recoveries come from connecting with the Divine and accessing the information required to bring life and health back. But it's completely unnecessary to nearly die in order to realize the truth about our Souls and our connection to the Divine. We have the power to work with this while we're still here.

That's my goal in this book. I'm going to teach you how to work with all of you—body, Soul, mind, and Spirit—in a way that helps you create your own personal heaven on earth so that you can truly enjoy your life and live it to the fullest. In short, I'm going to help you make your life easy—on all levels. Starting now.

CHAPTER 2

You Are an Eternal Being Whose Soul Never Dies

We are travelers on a cosmic journey—stardust, swirling and dancing in the eddies and whirlpools of infinity. Life is eternal. . . . We have stopped for a moment to encounter each other, to meet, to love, to share. This is a precious moment, but it is transient. It is a little parenthesis in eternity.

— DEEPAK CHOPRA

The first thing you need to know if you truly want your life to be easy is that you are much more than your body. You are actually a Soul that has lived many lifetimes and will live many more. You have been reincarnated time and time again in order to learn how to bring Spirit into matter. Your high-vibration Divine self is learning to dance in the clay by entering the densest substance in the universe—matter. The ultimate goal is to become a Divine co-creator right here on earth. The path that we follow in order to do this is set out by our Soul, to bring us closer to our Source. Each lifetime we live brings with it new lessons that aim to help us reach conscious union with the Divine part of ourselves, which is God. Everyone eventually reaches this goal of enlightenment, but there are certainly different levels of consciousness operating here on earth.

By fully understanding that we are immortal and that our current experience is simply a continuation for our Souls, we can get a better grasp of what it takes to make life easy. It will help us understand why we face certain challenges and what we can do to solve them. It will also open us up to connecting with our Soul's path, so we can gain insight about what will take us further on our journey toward enlightenment and union with God. These two things help bring us peace and health in this lifetime.

This Is Not Your First Rodeo

Let's begin with reincarnation, because when you consider reincarnation as the truth of our existence, your life improves on all levels.

Many people have questioned the fact of reincarnation, but there are so many extraordinary examples that it's becoming harder and harder to argue against. I have a friend whose oldest daughter died in a fire at about the age of eight. After several years, my friend had another baby girl. When this child could talk, she said to her mother, "I was Kayla and I died in a fire. Now I'm back." Mothers who have had abortions have heard similar things from their children. "When I came to you and Dad before, it wasn't time. But now it is." Stories of children remembering their past lives abound.

The important thing about reincarnation, on an emotional level, is that it helps you understand, deal with, and ultimately heal the thorny issues you face in this current lifetime—including challenges associated with your social status, your family, the deaths of loved ones, and your health. Each of these circumstances is actually chosen for you by your Soul to help you move forward toward enlightenment.

We have all had thousands of lifetimes. And the people you're around have been with you before—particularly family members, who are often your biggest challenges. My friend Dr. Gladys McGarey has long taught about reincarnation and the work of Edgar Cayce. One time when two of her children were fighting, she said, "Remember, you both chose this family." Pointing at his brother, her son said, "Yes, but I didn't know HE was going to be here!"

While understanding the challenges and painful circumstances you experience—especially those that elude the understanding of intellect—will not prevent you from hurting, it will give meaning and therefore comfort when facing them. I once heard of a Buddhist teacher who taught that there are legions of Souls lined up waiting for the privilege of being born into a body here on earth. There's no other place in the universe that is such a profound "Spirit into matter" playground where we practice bringing light into darkness. Imagine—a long line of Souls eager to have the very experience you are now having. Even if it's painful. To make life easy, you have to know that being here in a body, even if that body is sick, or taking care of someone who is sick, is not some kind of punishment for being bad, meted out by some judgmental God who is separate from you. That's a profound misunderstanding.

Truly heartbreaking things like a stillbirth, childhood cancer, or the loss of one's parents while still young could be severely traumatizing if there were nothing more to them than the experience itself. But by understanding the deeper meaning within these events, we are far better able to transform the grief and sadness that come with the inevitable losses that are part of being human. If you don't take this long view, you can spend a lifetime beating yourself up with anger and blame. For example, on a recent trip to my childhood home, I visited the cemetery where the Northrup family is buried and heard a story about an infant relative who had died at the turn of the 20th century. This child was the only son of an ancestor of mine, and he died when he was just a year old. His father spent the rest of his life blaming God for this loss. He never recovered from it.

The human heart and mind simply can't get over senseless losses like this unless we ask our Souls and God to help us see a bigger picture. If we don't, we are destined to go through life believing that our fate is determined simply by luck—good or bad.

And frankly, that approach makes life on earth a living hell. If we don't take the long view, we also miss the lessons we were supposed to learn in this lifetime, so we'll just have to come back into body and work on it again—only next time it will be harder.

Anything you face has been put there for a reason. Your Soul is showing you the emotional work necessary to bring light into the dark places. You came here to master life on earth and raise your vibration. And you won't be able to do that without reaching for assistance from the Divine (God) to help. Otherwise you will be lost.

Finding Solace

Understanding that we are Souls rather than bodies takes on a whole new meaning when we experience the death of someone close to us. When I was doing my residency in ob/gyn in Boston, I received a phone call that shattered my world. My younger sister Cindy was killed in a car accident on her way back from teaching a gymnastics class in Buffalo, New York.

Cindy was 23 years old and had just graduated from the University of Alaska with a degree in physical education. She was a free spirit who went to three different colleges without a single worry about how bad that might look on her resume. After the two of us took a long-awaited trip to Europe, I went to medical school and Cindy went back to Alaska to work on the famed Alaska Pipeline. She lived in the shipping crate of a bulldozer that had been made into a cabin. She regaled us with stories of careening through newly built sections of the pipeline on those wheeled carts you lie on to work on the underbody of a car—with the music of Pink Floyd blasting through the pipe via speakers placed at each end. She was such a force of light and fun, her death hit all of us really hard.

Shortly after Cindy's death, my mother ended up in the parking lot of a spiritualist church run by a friend of a friend. As she tells it, she barely knows how she got there. When she went into the service, the minister, who communed with spirits, said from the altar, "There's someone here whose name begins with a C. She wants her mother to know that she is okay. And that her granny was with her in the car." (My mother's mother—my granny—had died of a heart attack while shoveling snow about nine months before my sister was killed.)

My mother was so reassured by this one statement that she made arrangements for the minister, Margarete Haney, to come to her home for a special channeling session. I was in Boston at the time, but my sister Penny watched as Ms. Haney went into a trancelike state and her features and voice changed completely. A man's voice came out of her mouth. He introduced himself as Dr. Andre, and he spoke to us about my sister's death. He told us she had felt no pain and wasn't alone at the time of her passing. He also said that she was now safe and happy on the other side. My family made a tape recording of that session, and I'll never forget listening to it. There is no doubt that a Soul named Dr. Andre took over Ms. Haney's body for the purpose of teaching and healing. Dr. Andre helped all of us cope with the loss of our sister. He also helped us realize that she wasn't really dead. She had just left her body.

Sensing the Presence of the Past

Aside from helping you deal with pain and loss, accepting reincarnation can also help explain inexplicable things that are happening in your current lifetime. For example, when the first edition of my first book, *Women's Bodies, Women's Wisdom*, came out, I would often wake up screaming in the middle of the night, certain that someone was in the house with a gun and a plan to kill me. Ask my daughters. They were terrified. But not as terrified as I was. What I figured out was that I—probably like many of you reading this—had been burned at the stake as a witch on more than one occasion. Luckily, in this lifetime I haven't been killed for my holistic approach to women's health, but I've had more than my share of brushes with authority figures in my profession—most of whom were also my inquisitors in the past.

I have talked with countless women who have also felt "irrational" fears when faced with speaking their truth to authority figures. We sometimes joke about all the ways we have been silenced. This is not mere fantasy. After all, nine million women healers and midwives—as well as the men who supported them and the men who were healers themselves—were burned at the stake in the 1400s after two inquisitors issued the infamous document *Malleus Maleficarum* (Latin for *The Hammer of Witches*), identifying who the witches were. And as far as I can tell, it was any woman (or man) who used the medicine of the earth or his or her own intuitive gifts to heal.

So how does the past come into the present? The famous British biologist Rupert Sheldrake speaks of a "morphic field" of energy and information that exists outside of time and space. This field is a record of everything that has ever happened on the planet. Sometimes this information manifests in our lives as fears, anxieties, or even illnesses. Luckily, if you are able to recognize the influence of the past, the symptom you are experiencing can lead you to its cure—and to a clearing of the morphic field.

Many years ago, my mother developed intermittent pain in her abdomen. Rather than go to a doctor, which she intuitively knew wouldn't help, she had the feeling that she needed to drive across the country to visit my sister. There was something about that pilgrimage that spoke to her.

As she drove, the pain got worse and worse. At one point it got so bad she had to stop the car and pull her knees up to her chest. She actually thought she was spitting up blood. But there was nothing there. And then she had a vision—a flashback—that was as real to her as if it were happening that moment. She was a Viking with a sword. And she plunged the sword into the belly of a pregnant woman, killing both the baby and the woman. And in that moment—in present time—she realized that she was having the experience of both the perpetrator (the Viking) and the woman he had killed with the sword. The sword went right into the very place where she had been feeling the pain. She was overcome with grief about what she, as a Viking, had done.

The agony of guilt and remorse continued. When she got to my sister's house, she did a ritual with a local shaman. She wrote down everything about the incident she could think of. Then, on a full-moon night, she burned the paper and buried the ashes. Then she slept for hours. When she woke up all the pain and the grief were gone. She had somehow "cleansed" some past energy—and cleared some karma. My mother told me that she knew beyond a shadow of a doubt that if she hadn't let herself experience this entire process, from start to finish, she would have ended up with a deadly gastrointestinal disease. I am certain that she is correct.

Interestingly, on the drive back across the country, she stopped to see a relative. During the visit, he took her into his bedroom and said that there was something he wanted her to have. He handed her a three-foot statue. Of a Viking. With a sword.

Clearing the Morphic Field of the Past

That kind of story is almost never written about in conventional medical circles. Yet over the years, I have learned that indeed health and illness and trauma and recovery are far more mysterious than we have ever been led to believe. If you think the only things that make you sick are germs or injury, think again. The morphic field has a magnetic pull. It's the law of attraction in which like attracts like. Or birds of a feather flock together. This is a consistent universal law, and it will keep presenting the same circumstances over and over until we bring love and understanding to them. Then the morphic field changes and the point of attraction changes as well.

In order to truly make life easy, it's important to heal the wounds of the past—whether you were victim or persecutor (because we've all been both). You cannot simply dismiss inexplicable illnesses or feelings. They could be signs from your Soul that it's time for a healing. Our Souls are always trying to heal negative patterns within us, so they bring them up for clearing and healing. Sometimes that healing is a conscious choice in the moment, and sometimes it's a lifelong calling. I once went to see a woman who helps individuals heal and deal better with life by combining numerology, astrology, and the ancient Hebrew mystical system known as the Kabbalah. I was telling her how wonderful the pelvic surgeon was who was going to remove a fibroid I had in my uterus. I had sent him many patients and he did everything in his power to repair pelvic organs, not remove them. Her response was, "I wonder what he did to the pelvis in a past life." She was implying that in this life his amazing dedication to the health of women's pelvic organs was some kind of atonement or balance for deeds of the past.

Looking to the deeds of your past lives as causes for the problems in your current life is quite a leap for some people, but it's becoming more acceptable. For many years, people have understood this as a possibility, but they didn't share the information for fear of being judged as delusional. I remember years ago reading Dr. Raymond Moody's account of children who had had near-death experiences. Many were left with extraordinary gifts as a result—like photographic memories or the ability to compose amazing music. Or a lifelong connection with a spirit guide. However, most of the time, these same individuals, when they shared what had really happened, were told they were "imagining things." And thus they stopped sharing their experiences and kept it all to themselves. So much wonder is lost in a culture that believes only what it can see and measure with the five senses.

But sooner or later—and I'm hoping sooner rather than later—everyone will realize that their Souls have always been Divinely guiding them. The Soul is a force that is far greater than intellect. Call it inner guidance, call it a hunch or a feeling that results in goose bumps—whatever you call it, your job is to *call upon it* for assistance and guidance. We are born with this inner guidance, and it's always there, directing us toward accomplishing what our Souls came here to accomplish. Whatever you call it, there are some very specific ways in which you can learn to work with this Soul voice consciously.

Past-Life Regressions

One of the most powerful tools I've found for tapping into the experiences of the past in order to heal the present is the past-life regression. You can do these on your own using audio products, such as those by noted past-life regression therapist Brian Weiss, M.D., a Harvard-trained psychiatrist. There are also quite a lot of good books on the topic, including those by Dr. Weiss. David Wells of Portsmouth, England, who is a very skilled astrologer and Kabbalist, has also written some excellent books on past-life work. The extraordinary book *Repetition: Past Lives, Life, and Rebirth* by Doris E. Cohen, Ph.D., truly helps you put together the story of your past life by noticing the patterns that are repeating themselves in your current life.

My colleague Bob Fritchie, founder of the World Service Institute and author of *Being at One with the Divine* and *Divine Love Self Healing: The At Oneness System*, points out that individuals who don't respond to the usual Divine Love healing system (which is explored more in the next chapter) are often stuck because of past-life issues. Fear keeps many people from looking into the past, but you can easily access your past without fear if you align with your Spirit and Divine Love. To do this, close your eyes and use this petition from *Divine Love Self Healing:* "With my internal Spirit and Divine Love, I go backwards in time to the instance or instances that explain my current (name your problem) fully." After saying the petition, take a deep breath in through your nose. Hold it for a count of four. Then pulse it out like you're blowing your nose. You will usually get images of the situations that are causing the problem. And as Fritchie points out, it is nearly always an unloving action from the past that separated you from the Divine. That separation becomes the Soul debt that is carried forward into this lifetime. That Soul slate can be wiped clean by releasing blame and judgment and replacing them with self-acceptance and love.

While doing self-work is great, working with a reputable past-life regression therapist can also be helpful. To find someone, I suggest that you ask around. Get a recommendation. Very often, the minute you decide you're ready for something like this, you'll be introduced to a good resource. That's how easy life can be when you align with your Soul and the Divine.

A Blueprint of Your Soul's Intent

Viewing yourself as a Soul embodied over many lifetimes as part of a greater journey is helpful in ways beyond simply giving meaning to pain. It also opens your eyes to the fact of your Soul's journey itself. Knowing that you're working toward something, and understanding that you are on a path, gives you the opportunity to look at that path in order to traverse it more skillfully. An astrologic chart—read by a skilled astrologer—is one of the handiest tools I know of to do this.

Your astrologic chart is a map of what the heavens were doing at the moment you took birth—and that moment was chosen by your Soul before you even took your first breath. It is also a map of your Soul's journey through time. It will give you a very good idea of what you came here to do and be.

Your astrologic chart comprises the pattern of planets in the sky—both above and below the horizon—at the moment of your birth. It describes your tendencies, characteristics, challenges, and potential. It also can give you some very concrete information about your past lives' challenges and what your Soul came to do this time around. This information is found in what are called the nodes of the moon—the south and the north nodes. The south node gives you information about where you've been. The north node tells you where you're going and what you came here to master.

Keep in mind, what I'm talking about here is not the kind of astrology you see in newspapers and magazines. These horoscopes are sun-sign astrology, which is nothing more than an interesting parlor game. Newspaper columns with sun-sign readings started in the 20th century as a way to sell more newspapers. But the sun sign is just one aspect of your individual astrologic signature, and it won't give you much information if you don't know the rest of your chart as well.

A complete horoscope includes the moon sign, the sun sign, the rising sign, a series of planets, the nodes of the moon, and often some asteroids. Your sun sign (Libra, Aries, Gemini) is only a very small part of your total horoscope. Still, your sun sign can tell you a few things—astrologer Daniel Giamario calls our sun the fuel we use to accomplish our current life purpose. So, if you are a Capricorn sun, you are quite likely to be practical and down-to-earth depending upon where all the other planets are and what influence they are having.

There are many different types of astrology—evolutionary, sun sign, shamanic, Vedic, and Venus Star Point, to name a few—and each of these can help you learn something different about your path.

Averting Astrology Fears

Many people will look at their charts or their horoscopes and ask, "Is it bad?" But this question doesn't ever need to be asked, because the answer is always no. Astrology is simply a tool—it has no power other than what you give it. It's like checking the weather forecast to see if you should pack a raincoat. It does not tell you your fate. That, my friend, is entirely up to you. A horoscope suggests the plotline for the play you're acting in. But it doesn't tell you how to play your part, what to wear, or how it ends.

What astrology does is give you a road map for the journey of your Soul. It's designed to help you maximize access to your Soul's original blueprint. Every chart has its challenges and its gifts. But there are no "bad" charts.

While there is still a stigma against the use of astrology as guidance, that stigma has lessened even over the course of my lifetime. Years ago, when I had my first astrologic reading, the astrologer told me that someday she was going to have a cocktail party and invite all the doctors—my colleagues—who came to see her regularly. She said, "You are all going to be surprised at who is here." And from that, I learned that many people, including many very famous and successful people, use astrology. They just don't talk about it.

Over and over again, our overly intellectualized society steers us away from the very things that hold the power to reinforce our Soul's path and give our lives meaning. For years and years, my mainstream publishers said to me, "Please don't talk about astrology, it turns people off." And so I kept it quiet (mostly) during my "trying to fit in" years. But those years are over.

Many of those who discredit astrology have done no research on it. As Rob Brezsny, an astrologer and the author of *Pronoia Is the Antidote for Paranoia*, so brilliantly states, "They haven't read smart astrological philosophers like Dane Rudhyar, don't know that seminal astronomer Johannes Kepler was a skilled astrologer, and aren't aware that eminent psychologist C. G. Jung cast horoscopes and believed that 'astrology represents the summation of all the psychological knowledge of antiquity.' The closest approach the fraudulent 'skeptics' usually make to the ancient art is to glance at a tabloid horoscope column. To match their carelessness, I might make a drive-by of a strip mall and declare that the profession of architecture is shallow and debased."

Getting a Reading

As I noted when we began talking about astrology, an astrologic chart can be extremely helpful *when read by a skilled astrologer*. I wish I could say that this is something you can do on your own, but to truly understand what's happening in an astrological chart takes years of study. It is an art. So your best bet when trying to tap into the wisdom of astrology is to work with someone who has been referred to you. Someone who has been doing readings for years. Don't simply walk into a shop and hope for a good experience. Get recommendations. Do your research.

One thing to keep in mind when you're looking for a trustworthy person to work with is to avoid doom-and-gloom astrologers. These people have a tendency to share information in a way that is seriously disempowering. Too many people have been "hexed" by astrologers who read charts as though they are warnings from the Divine. One of my friends had a reading in which an astrologer told her that she shouldn't work with groups because she had no skills in that area. Trust me, there was nothing in her chart that indicated anything of the sort. Part of your Soul's journey will be discovering astrologers, psychics, and other guides who can help you along your way.

Understanding Transits: Saturn, Uranus, and Chiron

While reading a chart fully is best left to a skilled professional, there are some universal truths reflected in astrology that will help you understand challenges you face at certain times of your life. Certain planetary alignments affect all of us in similar ways, and often these alignments happen at specific times in all of our lives. Three of the most powerful to keep in mind as you move through the years have to do with Saturn, Uranus, and Chiron.

- **Saturn:** Saturn is all about respecting and working within limits and boundaries. Saturn Return, which refers to the time when the planet Saturn returns to the location it was at when you were born, occurs for most people between the ages of 28 and 32 and then again at around age 58. A Saturn Return means that it's time to grow up. Adolescence is over. It's time to become an adult and figure out how to survive on your own. The first Saturn Return is often accompanied by some kind of loss or trauma that forces us to wake up. Some individuals don't make it. There's even something called the 27 Club, which refers to a group of musicians who all died at age 27. These include Kurt Cobain, Jim Morrison, Janis Joplin, Brian Jones, and Jimi Hendrix. The second

Saturn Return is when our Souls urge us to move from survival mode to thriving.

- **Uranus:** Uranus is known as the great awakener, and it's all about breaking through limits. It gives us the opportunity to soar rather than dive. To break the rules and color outside the lines. The Uranus Opposition happens at about the age of 42, and this is when the "family trance" that we were born into begins to crumble away as our Souls say, "Wait. Is this all there is?" The Uranus Opposition is a big wake-up call to live your own authentic life—not the one chosen for you by your parents or employer. Our culture calls it a midlife crisis. And many women simply blame it on menopause. But it's a far bigger deal than that. It's a spiritual awakening orchestrated by your Soul and the universe. Uranus also makes an appearance around the ages of 21, 63, and 84. While these transits present us with circumstances that are designed to liberate us from the status quo, the Uranus Opposition is the major event with Uranus.

- **Chiron:** Chiron, the Wounded Healer, also makes one big return in our lives. The Chiron Return comes at about the age of 52, and it presents us with a situation that tests us in the aspect of our lives where we are skilled enough to help everyone else but can't seem to get it together ourselves. This event often makes us feel like we are dying. And we are. We're dying to our old way of being. And if we try to hang on, we're likely to get sick. During Chiron Return, it's time to trust our Souls and move ahead in faith.

The Soul's Journey

Understanding the true immortal nature of yourself—understanding that your Soul is on a journey through many lifetimes—is a powerful tool in your efforts to make life easy. Knowing that there are universal forces acting on us in ways that are beyond our ability to control can help us bring meaning to our lives. Working with these forces consciously, through practices such as past-life regression and astrology, gives us the ability to live our lives with maximum effectiveness and fulfillment. It gives us the chance to learn the lessons we need to learn. And those lessons are pretty simple: to bring love, forgiveness, and understanding to the areas of our lives where it hasn't yet been. And also to stop living in fear. This includes loving and forgiving yourself.

We are all making our way to union with the Divine, and yet we exist on this mortal plane. The place of matter. The densest place in the universe. When we bring more light and love here, it changes the entire universe, helping it evolve. That's a huge service to "all that is," don't you think? Merging these two realities and working skillfully within them is the most important, fulfilling, and practical work we can ever do.

CHAPTER 3

Communicating with the Divine

Communicating with God is the most extraordinary experience imaginable, yet at the same time it's the most natural one of all, because God is present in us at all times. Omniscient, omnipotent, personal—and loving us without conditions. We are connected as One through our divine link with God.

— Eben Alexander

For centuries, we've been led to believe that only a few chosen people could talk to God. Only those who had mystical experiences or conversed with burning bushes. Mere mortals didn't have this ability. And thus, entire populations have been controlled by a few—many of whom just exploited the trust that was placed in their hands. You know who I'm talking about so I won't go into it.

But we all have the ability to communicate directly with God, and your relationship with the Divine is, in fact, one of the most important ways to make your life easy. Establishing a direct connection with God, the Creator, will provide you with support that you can't get anywhere else. It will help you move forward on your Soul's journey, and it will give you somewhere to turn when things seem hopeless or out of control.

I remember one night years ago, when I called on God with my entire being.

First, a little background. My colleagues and I had started Women to Women, a new model for women's health care back in the 1980s. Before Women to Women, the health-care model we were working in didn't focus on healing as a measure of success. Though all my colleagues were devoted physicians, the system in which we found ourselves tended to focus on how many surgeries you did and how many patients you saw. Getting to the root of someone's problem—for example, sexual abuse—was generally not addressed, simply because the system wasn't (and still isn't) set up to deal with this quickly.

One of my female colleagues sustained a hip fracture when we were working in this environment, and during her convalescence she drew a cartoon that pretty much summarized the dilemma we were all facing. The cartoon was of a gravestone, and on it were the words "Here lies JCG" (not her real initials). Underneath that were listed the office stats by which our "worth" and productivity were measured: OVI (office visit initial): 9,326; NOB (new OB patients): 7,390; C-sections: 4,500. The image was a stark summary of the belief system running our day-to-day lives.

I knew something had to change. I had a vision of a new kind of practice that would honor the wisdom of women's bodies. I also envisioned it in a homelike setting where women would feel comfortable and where their entire stories would be valued. Two nurse practitioners had started the original Women to Women nearby, and we decided to join forces, put our money where our mouths were instead of complaining, and create a new kind of health care. So we bought an old Victorian home and made the bedrooms into exam rooms and the closets into changing areas. And when women came to see us, they'd sit down on the couches in our offices and just weep with relief. Finally, a place where all of them—body, mind, and Spirit—was honored and listened to.

The problem was not only that none of us knew anything about business but also that, in moving toward our new vision, we had taken all of our old beliefs with us. And the consciousness of our patients hadn't changed much either. This led to unrealistic expectations of us as healers. Wasn't there a pill or procedure that could heal the pain of sexual abuse, divorce, fear of cancer, or shame? No wonder the old model rewarded doing more surgery. Or just writing a prescription. The long and short of it was that we found ourselves struggling to pay the bills, let alone pay ourselves, unless we retreated to much of what we had tried to leave.

The night I called to God I had been working late and it was after dark when I finally finished the pile of charts on my desk. I had pretty much had it with the rigors of medical practice, the late nights on call, and the fact that very few of my patients seemed to want to know how intimately their minds, bodies, and Souls were connected. They just wanted a pill to fix them. I was afraid of the disapproval of my mainstream colleagues and the disapproval of the medical board. My own husband at the time didn't even see the value of my contribution.

So I stood in the dark doorway of our center and looked up at the stars, saying aloud, "Please help me get it right this time. I don't want to come back and do this again." I was imploring God to help me see my way out of my dilemma—to show me how to learn the lesson I came to learn and make the contribution I said I would make before I was born. I didn't know how to communicate directly with the Creator back then. But I knew for sure that it was possible. I also knew that praying to God and asking for support and help was the only way out of my dilemma. I knew that my work had been a Soul choice more than anything else. I had promised my Soul that I would teach what I knew to be true in this lifetime. It's just that it wasn't easy. Not even a little. Many people certainly didn't want to hear my truth. Still, it made all the difference to know for sure that my strength and help lay in my connection with the Creator rather than simply myself.

Soon thereafter, I stood at my bedside table and said a prayer out loud inspired by Florence Scovel Shinn. It was this: "Infinite Spirit, give me a sign. Show me the next best use of my gifts and talents." It was 11 A.M. on a Friday. At 2 P.M. that same day, I got a call from a friend who is a literary agent. He said, "I think you should write a book." Bingo! I was off and running.

And that book, *Women's Bodies, Women's Wisdom*, not only articulated a language of women's health—everything that can go right with the female body—but also allowed me to reach millions of women all over the world with what I know to be true. And it sincerely and profoundly helped so many people. The response was a miracle. It also opened up a world of joy and fulfillment far beyond anything I could have ever created for myself without God.

Connecting with God

Initiating a connection with the Creator can be as simple as saying, "Help me! I'm clueless" when you're faced with a dilemma of any kind and you don't know what to do. But you don't need a dilemma in order to connect with God. Just say "Thank you" when you see a glorious sunset that brings you to your knees in wonder. I have felt the presence of God many times in the delivery room when a newborn cries for the first time. Everyone in the room is transfixed with the wonder of it.

You can connect with the Divine deliberately through prayers or a petition such as "I accept Divine Love" or by asking for a sign—like I did—and then seeing what shows up. Connecting with the Creator might involve religious services with other like-minded individuals. Few things in life feel more holy than singing joyful praise songs to God at the top of your lungs in the company of others. Especially when the musicians are skilled. But it sure doesn't require this. Not in the least. Don't let anyone tell you otherwise.

You may think the Divine is not as important as all the other things in your life. But nothing could be *more* important. In her magnificent book *Outrageous Openness: Letting the Divine Take the Lead*, Tosha Silver writes, "What if God *is* the story?" Indeed. God, of which we are all a part, *is* the whole story. And when you put your relationship with this Divine part of yourself first, everything else falls into place. When you put this relationship first, you get reassurance, guidance, and wisdom that is always there for you no matter what else is happening in your life. Nothing can replace a one-on-one relationship with the Source that created you. Absolutely nothing. Not fame, not money, not a lover. Nothing. Your relationship with the Divine is the one and only thing you can absolutely count on. And it is the only thing that will continually bring you wonder. And mystery. And steadfast trust and joy. Everything else comes and goes.

The Ego

We talked a little bit about the ego in Chapter 1. It can be your friend or your foe. It is the only thing that gets in the way of you realizing your relationship with the Divine. It's that pesky doubting Thomas inside your head that makes all kinds of excuses for not connecting with the Divine. However, once you understand how to work with it consciously, it holds the key to creating heaven on earth. It becomes a co-creative partner.

As we talk about ego, I have to stress again that your ego is not bad. The ego gets a very bad rap in spiritual circles. We're taught that we should somehow transcend it or get rid of it. That it is responsible for all our suffering. And though this is true on one level, your ego is absolutely necessary for you to develop Self. What do I mean by this? Self—with a capital S—means the true unique nature of you. Every aspect of you—both Divine and on the physical plane. That includes your personality. Your ego brings this unique combination of Spirit and Soul into a very specific package designed to create your life experience. That would be you. You can't get rid of the ego—you need it to live in your current embodied state, as an individual who is separate from others.

The formation of our ego begins in childhood by what we are rewarded for, what we learn from our parents, what we do for work, how old we are, how much we weigh, and so on. The ego thinks in terms of good and bad. Though it appears to keep us safe—and it actually does on some level—it also keeps us locked in to the illusion that our problems will all be solved by getting the right people to like us, more money, the right lover, the right house, the right wardrobe, and so many other material things. It also thinks it's supposed to be able to figure everything out on its own. Otherwise it is weak. This is why *ego* is often said to be an acronym for "edging God out."

The ego serves a very important purpose despite all this. Its real job is to take direction from our Souls for how to create our individual versions of heaven on earth. If you don't have an ego that's healthy and strong enough to take on the tasks for which you were born, then you're not going to get very far along your Soul's journey. But if you can allow your ego to take orders from your Soul, you're often provided with circumstances that are far more satisfying than anything your ego could come up with left on its own. In other words, left without God.

Getting Your Ego to Cooperate

So what to do? You have to understand where your ego comes from and what it really represents. The most compassionate, caring, and practical approach to the ego I've found comes from Matt Kahn, a spiritual teacher, empath, and author of *Whatever Arises, Love That*. Matt points out that the ego arises from an overstimulated nervous system.

When we are born, our consciousness is pure love, and our nervous systems are generally calm. (Hence the phrase "Sleep like a baby.") When infants encounter a new stimulus, they cry. The same thing happens when they experience a wet diaper or hunger. Movement, sound, and tears are the ways in which our nervous systems were designed to digest the stresses of life. It's not just true of human babies; all animals do this automatically. After a gazelle has been chased by a lion, it shakes. After women give birth, they shake. This shaking calms us down and burns off excess stress hormones.

With each stimulus, the nervous system of a baby produces a spike of energy and then returns to its natural state of pure loving consciousness. Over time, however, as these energy spikes become more frequent with the inevitable new experiences of life, the subconscious mind makes a decision. To conserve energy and maintain a more steady state, it's just easier for the nervous system to stay at a higher state of stimulation. And this is the birth of the ego—this is when we develop thought patterns and ideas to maintain the higher state of stimulation in response to our circumstances. Sadly, in this higher state of overstimulation the baby no longer reverts easily to pure loving consciousness. Over time the subconscious mind makes a decision that this overstimulated state is the new "normal"—a distorted condition that takes us away from our innate loving consciousness—and thus the ego is fortified. It is solidly in place to protect us and help us maneuver through the obstacles we face.

The formation of the ego is dependent on the environment in which we grow up. We are all part of tribes—groups of people with shared beliefs and values. Some of these are recognized by our Souls as helpful. However, some of these beliefs and values feel absolutely wrong. But we have to fit in to survive. And if we don't fit in, we risk being shamed, abandoned, or betrayed. These three wounds are, according to the research of neuropsychologist Mario Martinez, the three primal wounds that all tribes all over the world use to punish their members who stray outside the tribal belief systems. If a tribal belief runs counter to what your Soul knows to be true, then living this lie in order to fit into your tribe further overstimulates your nervous system, adding power to your ego's beliefs about the world. Here's an example: "In this family, everyone becomes a lawyer. There's no way we're supporting you if want to be a musician." The Soul of the musician is at odds with the dictates of the tribe. And so she is at risk for abandoning herself and her Soul requirements in order to give in to the tribe. But once she resolves this issue by aligning with the Divine, she finds the love and power within to follow her heart and the dictates of her Soul. (The tribe usually doesn't like this, but the Soul cheers!)

Or we could look at the dictates of a religion. What if you experienced two things in your youth: (1) a deep knowing that you are gay and (2) constant ideological reminders that being gay is a sin against God? Imagine the overstimulation of the nervous system arising from this. You have to keep your core identity secret. Shame sets in. You start to believe that you *are* a mistake.

We develop ego strategies that work to shield us from feeling the pain of this separation from our true natures as we try to fit in with our tribes. Over time our consciousness gets limited through patterns of overstimulation, such that the nervous system actually deletes anything that contradicts our most dearly held beliefs about what is required for us to feel safe and to fit in.

So as you can see, our tribes contribute to hefty egos emotionally, but they also do so physically. The shame, abandonment, and betrayal we experience produce small amounts of inflammatory chemicals throughout our bodies. This conditions our nervous, endocrine, and immune systems to remain in hypervigilant states from childhood on. This in turn can create illness, which also influences and shapes our understanding of who we are in the world.

In my experience, susceptibility to illness is very much determined by the agenda of your Soul. When you don't listen to the dictates of your Soul regularly, it will get your attention through your health. It's the old "If you don't listen the first time, you get hit with a bigger hammer" approach. By the way, this has absolutely nothing to do with punishment for being "bad." It is simply the way your Soul staged the play that you're acting in this time around.

There Is a Divine Purpose to All of This

The good news is that as consciousness expands, our old beliefs dissolve and a new life is revealed. We don't need to experience illness or accidents as a reset button. But if we do experience them, it doesn't mean we've done something wrong—and hence are to blame. That's the first place the ego always goes. And if you keep going there, your life won't be easy. Maybe not for lifetimes.

Please remember that all this ego development and even childhood wounding serve a Divine purpose. The overstimulated nervous system of your childhood acts like a psychological cocoon, guarding the sleeping butterfly of your original innocence. Meanwhile, your ego helps you develop the skills and experience you need to accomplish your Soul's mission—the Divine adventure you are on. When you recognize your overstimulated nervous system for what it is, you no longer take what happens to you so personally. You observe it. Unconditionally. And you become fascinated by how your world opens up as you relax. Like a flower. Petal by petal. Organically, in its own time.

Matt Kahn writes in *Whatever Arises, Love That*: "No matter how many years you have spent immersed in spiritual discourse, the living realization of truth cannot be fully revealed until the nervous system is relaxed. Even on a mystical level, the degree to which a nervous system relaxes also determines who sees angels, ghosts, alternate dimensions, or even receives intuitive messages."

In Chapter 5, I'll teach you how to deal with your emotions and why emotions are absolutely key to getting the ego to a place where it serves you rather than keeps you in bondage. But here's a hint: When you are moved to tears or to anger or to laughter, know that this is a sign that your nervous system is relaxing. Many of us have been taught to hide strong emotions. And yes, there is a time and a place to express them. But be clear on this: When something moves you emotionally, it's a sure sign that you are on the right track.

God Communication 101

Now that you understand the obstacle of the ego, it's time to get in touch with the Divine. As you're striving to communicate, remember that God is a loving presence, mediated through your Spirit and your Soul. It's possible for each and every one of us to communicate directly with God, like we're sitting down and having a cup of coffee together. It's that simple.

As you've already learned, your Spirit and your Soul are two aspects of you that are actually God within you. Another thing that's helpful to know is that most of who you really are isn't even in your physical body! That's right—most of you is nonphysical. When you establish a relationship with God, what you're really doing is talking to the nonphysical aspect of yourself. The part of God that comes through you as you. The Self, as it were. Or Higher Self or Higher Power. You are establishing communication between the Self who is down here in a body, and the Greater Self who is guiding you through the mastery course that is life.

You've probably heard the phrase "Ask and it is given," right? Well, that is pretty much how communicating with God works. You first have to ask—sincerely and honestly—for help. And then release your resistance to the answer, because the answer is always there waiting for you. The reason we don't always recognize that is because the answers are usually vibrating on a higher plane than the one we are in when we ask the question. Keep this in mind. Inspiration from a higher source can't reach you when you are in the low vibration of states like anger, sadness, and fear. To make life easy, we have to get out of our own way as we seek to get in touch with the Creator. This is the primary task of being in a body in the first place. Asking is the prayer. Intuition, or your inner guidance, is the answer.

So you must ask and then listen. Send your prayer and trust what comes to you in response. Don't let your ego block communication. You were born with a direct channel to Source, but ego can get in the way. And ego becomes stronger the older you get. There's a story about a little boy whose mother overhears him saying to his baby brother, "Please tell me about God. I'm starting to forget."

Remember that the ego is formed from an overstimulated nervous system and a mind that then makes up stories about us and our circumstances. These beliefs operate at a subconscious level. They aren't readily accessible to our conscious minds, but they run our lives nevertheless. For example, if your mother is an alcoholic and doesn't know how to love and cherish herself, let alone you, you decide that you must be unlovable because she isn't there for you. That's not the truth at all. It's just something you made up to make logical sense of your circumstances. The only way out of this common dilemma and all the others like it is to make a conscious connection with your Divinity.

Loving Your Ego Away

When you connect with the Divine through prayer or other means and then listen for guidance or support, you will likely be worried that the guidance you get is the voice of your ego and not your Soul. This makes you doubt the information that is coming to you. *Am I really hearing the Divine? Who am I to talk to God?* This is inevitable. It comes from growing up in a culture that, by and large, teaches us that we don't have access to inner guidance and must seek it from authority figures.

So when you first start communicating with the Divine, you'll probably think you're making up the answers. You aren't. But depending on your background and conditioning, it might take you a while to believe this.

When doubt appears, or you start to beat yourself up, just remember your ego is trying to protect you in the best way it knows how—usually by suggesting that you're "making it up" or are "too big for your britches" or whatever well-worn conditioning is familiar to you from your parents or other authority figures. Don't fight this. Instead, when the negative thoughts arrive, just say, "I love you for having this thought. Aren't you adorable?" Negativity from the ego can't live in an atmosphere of humor, acceptance, and light. It melts away like morning dew in the afternoon sun.

Remember this: The voice of the ego is filled with fear, doubt, self-loathing, judgment, shame, and guilt. Divine guidance *never* contains these qualities. And the only way to dismantle the ego is through love and confidence in the Divine. This develops over time, with intention. And simply by loving your innate innocence the way you would love any child in pain.

The guidance you receive when you ask for help via a petition or prayer is the Divine speaking to you. Over time, you'll learn to trust it. I always hear it in my left ear. So learn to be a good secretary. Just note what's being said that is supportive and kind. When that doubt slips in, acknowledge it, thank it for trying to help, kid around with it a bit, and then let it go. And also shake it off. Literally. Moving your body really helps.

Now let's get into some specific ways of communicating with God. Divine Love Petitions, Change Me Prayers, and Speaking with Angels are my favorite go-to practices for doing this. There are, of course, many others.

Divine Love Petitions

I quickly introduced you to Bob Fritchie and his Divine Love Petitions in Chapter 2 to help you look into your past, but now I want to go more deeply into his healing process because the Divine Love Petitions are the most all-purpose and practical way I've learned to connect with the Creator. Bob has worked for years to refine the Divine Love Healing Process, and the testimonials on his website about healing everything from obesity to pancreatic cancer are so uplifting!

Bob, an engineer who has done extensive studies on energy healing, points out that the body is a battery—an electromagnetic field of potential. Divine Love is distributed throughout our bodies almost instantaneously via the crystalline matrix of our connective tissue. A Divine Love Petition is basically a process of asking Spirit to direct Divine Love to a specific issue and then observing what happens. When you present the request to the Divine and ask for help, help is given. The process is outlined in the box that follows.

Divine Love Petitions

This process can be used to ask for guidance, healing, or help with anything you need. You simply have to adjust the petition to address the problem you are looking to solve.

1. Sit comfortably with your arms and legs uncrossed and remove all jewelry.

2. Prepare to draw in your breath through your nose right after you say the petition.

3. Say the following out loud: "With my Spirit and the angels' help [you can even name a specific angel] I focus Divine Love throughout my system. I ask my Spirit to identify any cause or any situation that separates me from the Creator. And remove those causes and situations with Divine Love, according to the Creator's will."

4. Breathe in through your nose, and hold your breath for a count of four. This brings the petition into your body.

5. Pulse your breath out through your nose like you are clearing your nose. This releases the petition to the universe.

6. Just sit quietly and focus on your thymus gland, which is right under your sternum—that place where you'd thump your chest and say "Oh my!" Divine Love is mediated to the rest of the body through this gland.

    What do you notice? Most people notice tingling in their chest or hands or somewhere in their bodies. Some notice a feeling of deep peace.

    If you get a pain somewhere or start to cough, just pulse your breath again. And send Divine Love to the area that is bothering you.

    Now you are connected with the Creator.

7. This is very simple. In silence, ask a question and just listen, or do a more specific petition to help you get answers: "With my Spirit and the angels' help, I focus Divine Love throughout my system, I acknowledge my [state the problem], and ask that I be shown what I need to know about this issue according to the Creator's will."

Draw in your breath through your nose. Hold it. Now pulse it out through your nose. Sit in silence for a minute or so. Imagine a door or a window opening and showing you what you need to know. Trust the image.

If you don't get an answer, do another petition to remove your blockages from getting an answer!

"With my Spirit and the angels' help, I ask that Divine Love show me what I need to know. And also heal this issue with Divine Love according to the Creator's will."

Remember, Divine Love and the Creator are *not* forces outside yourself that are judging you for being bad or good. Those are ego constructs, and many of them continue to influence us adversely from our childhood. So there are times when you need to simply say, "I now release this pattern with the help of Divine Love." Period. That way you're not expecting a Divine force outside of yourself to miraculously step in! Remember, it's all *you*.

8. Do a final petition to turn the entire issue over to the Creator. Just say, "I now turn this issue over to the Creator and ask that it be healed with Divine Love." (Or make up your own wording.)

Bob Fritchie suggests that you stay connected with Divine Love by having an intention to reconnect every time you go to the bathroom. Just say, "I now connect with Divine Love," and pulse your breath. Then you're back in touch! The truth is that we lose our connection to Divine Love every time that pesky nervous system overstimulation comes back on board. And every time we get scared or angry. That's why you have to practice staying connected.

When I use the Divine Love Petition process, I set the timer on my phone for two minutes. Then I sit in silence and simply pay attention to images that appear or songs that I hear. Yes—for me, songs are a very important part of my inner guidance.

The Divine Love Petition can be used in any area of your life where you're looking for guidance or need healing: health, business, relationships, and so on. You simply have to state the issue in your petition.

I have worked with my business partner Diane Grover for well over three decades. She was my first nurse, and she now runs the entire business. We have a profound soul connection. When I went into labor with my youngest daughter, she had a dream that she was giving birth, and then she went to the office to cancel all the patients that day because she just knew that I was in labor. When that same daughter had her first baby (my first grandchild), Diane woke up with abdominal cramps that lasted right up until my daughter delivered little Penelope!

Every weekday Diane and I meet over at the 100-year-old schoolhouse that is my office, and we practice applying Divine Love for our business. And sometimes on behalf of friends and family.

We start with an aspect of the business in which we need guidance or that has us concerned. Over the years, we have found that each of us gets images that are very specific and helpful in making business decisions. And we also clear the energy of the past on a regular basis. We use Divine Love Petitions for deciding whether or not to take on a specific project.

The petition goes something like this: "With our Spirits and the angels' help, we focus Divine Love throughout our systems. We acknowledge the upcoming trip to Denver [let's say], and we ask that our path be Divinely guided and that our Souls' journey be eased. With Divine Love according to the Creator's will." Then we pulse our breath and sit for two minutes, after which we share what we "saw." And also any song we heard. We often hear Bible verses that are relevant, as both of us grew up in Christian traditions and those texts still resonate with us.

Over time, this has developed our intuitive abilities a great deal, and it keeps us on track with our real mission on the planet so that we don't get distracted by all the treasures of the world that ultimately mean nothing. Sometimes, when asking about a specific project, we get the word *NO* on the inner screen of our mind. And sometimes there is a lesson to be learned from going ahead with a project that doesn't turn out like we wanted it to. For example, I worked for about two years, and at considerable expense, to try to come to a legal agreement with a group of businessmen who wanted me to serve as a spokesperson for a product they were selling. I was to be their "show pony." And at first I was flattered and excited to do it. But since one of my life lessons is ego development, this particular arrangement was never meant to bear fruit. Instead, it was designed to teach me how to stand on my own two feet—and eventually start my own company that sold a similar product.

So just because you don't always get the answers your ego wants to hear, that doesn't mean you're doing anything wrong!

Peeling the Onion

Healing with Divine Love is like peeling the layers of an onion. When it comes to health issues or thorny emotional issues, it can take a while to get your nervous system relaxed and to get to what's really causing your issue. But Divine Love helps enormously while you're going through the process.

When Bob Fritchie teaches the Divine Love Healing Process, he often shows a picture of an onion into which he has injected blue dye. When you peel the layers of the onion, you see that the dye has penetrated into the deepest layers of the onion. It is the same way with healing. It happens in layers. For example, this past summer I developed left-knee pain when I bent down into a squatting position. There was nothing wrong with the knee physically. I knew that because I was able to perform all my Pilates exercises as usual. As a physician, I knew that if there had been something structurally wrong, this wouldn't have been possible. Also, multiple sessions with fascial stretching, which is excellent for knee problems, and even acupuncture didn't work. The pain didn't go away with many Divine Love Petitions, even when I worked with Bob directly on this issue. Then one day I slipped on some black ice and injured my right leg. That resulted in a great deal of right-leg pain. Now I didn't have a leg to stand on. Literally. I knew that this was highly symbolic. So I did a petition to release my old way of moving forward in the world, making sure to say that I released this pattern with my own will. The pain in my right leg went away almost immediately. The left-knee problem abated somewhat but didn't go away completely.

The reason is that I was in the process of learning an entirely new way of moving forward in the world vis-à-vis the women in my life and my own feminine way of being. (The left side represents the mother, the women in our lives, and also our feminine side.) I had years and years of programming in this area that were slowly but surely leaving my body. One layer at a time.

If you're familiar with any of my other books, you know I had a large fibroid tumor in my uterus back in my perimenopausal years. I knew a lot about health and healing, having been a practicing ob/gyn for years by that point. I even knew that fibroids were "creativity that hadn't been birthed yet." What I didn't know was that they were also related to funneling creative energy into a dead-end job or relationship. In my case, my Soul—through my uterus—was giving me a very tangible example of exactly that. The fibroid grew to the size of a soccer ball. When I had it removed surgically, I asked the anesthesiologist to say the following as I went under: "And when you awaken, the pattern that created this will have left your body." Two years later, I was a single woman. I had been peeling the layers on that particular onion for about six years before I got the full message. And relationships of all kinds have been my teachers (and onion layers) for my entire life. Until I finally surrendered to the truth that is in this book. My primary relationship has to be with the Divine first. Everything else follows that!

Change Me Prayers

My good friend and colleague Tosha Silver, whose seminal book *Outrageous Openness: Letting the Divine Take the Lead* has changed the lives of many for the better, created Change Me Prayers and has written an entire book on them entitled *Change Me Prayers: The Hidden Power of Spiritual Surrender*. Basically a Change Me Prayer is a prayer from your ego to your Divine Self. Tosha says it's the answer to the question "How do you change a pattern that is persistent and that you've tried everything you know of to change?"

A Change Me Prayer goes like this.

> Divine Beloved, please change me into someone who is willing to receive.

> Divine Beloved, please change me into someone who can deeply and sincerely surrender my will to THY will and truly TRUST the Divine to take the lead.

> Divine Beloved, please change me into someone who truly knows her value and worth. I am yours, you are mine, we are One.

Tosha's teaching about "letting the Divine take the lead" is life changing. But in a crazy culture that brainwashes us into thinking we should be able to manifest whatever we want by making the right list, taking the right actions, and doing the right affirmations, it can be *very* difficult for the ego to let go of the reins. I call this the disease of "doership." After all, we've been taught from the time that we were little kids that success, love, health, and happiness were dependent on doing what our culture tells us to do. Even when it conflicts with what we know in our hearts is right.

Change Me Prayers are enormously helpful and practical for learning to trust ourselves and remove ourselves from the traps our egos set for us. The bottom line is this: The Divine has a plan for each of us. That plan is your destiny. You chose it before you were born. That Divine is inside you and talking to you constantly. Your job is to align with that plan and let it lead you. But very few people have been trained to listen for this guidance. So the basic Change Me Prayer is this: "Please change me into someone who trusts the Divine part of myself."

This takes practice. But over time you'll find that it works.

One more thing: Letting the Divine take the lead doesn't mean you sit around and wait for God to do the laundry. It means you remain open to the messages and inner prompting you receive and then take action on what you're shown.

Angelic Assistance

Since that day at the age of 12 when I excitedly read *Natives of Eternity*, angels have become much more mainstream, and that is truly a Godsend. The popularity of these guides has been spurred on by such authors as Doreen Virtue and Kyle Gray, who portray angels in such a different way than they are commonly depicted in Scripture. These teachers bring a wonderful energy and fresh perspective to the subject. For example, Kyle points out that angels are not always little cherubic creatures. They are fierce and powerful. Big guns, as it were. Angels are even becoming supporting pieces in books on much vaster subjects. Anthony William has helped heal thousands of people by listening to a voice in his head called Spirit of the Most High, which has defined itself to him as "the living word *compassion*." Anthony has an entire chapter on angelic help in his book *Medical Medium*, in which he lists the 21 Essential Angels who are here to help and then mentions that there are 144,000 unknown angels we can call on in addition. Anthony suggests calling on three or four angels at a time for whatever is bothering you.

I have always believed in the power of angelic help, and I've experienced it in my own life. We all have guardian angels, guiding us by the hand, even if we don't know it. We can always count on them to lead us in the right direction if we choose to listen. We can also call on them for help—we simply have to ask for it. But to make the connection with angelic help, you need to ask out loud! Your voice has a particular signature and resonance that the angels will hear. The words "and with the angels' help" were added to the petitions that Bob Fritchie created because Bob found that this made the petitions far more powerful.

So when you're facing something you're not sure how to deal with, simply ask for help. Why not, right? That's how we make life easy. That's how we create our own personal heaven on earth. And, as the late Peter Calhoun, an Episcopal priest turned shaman, said once in a workshop I attended, "When you're outmanned and outgunned, you've got to appeal to a higher authority." The angels are certainly that!

CHAPTER 4

Understanding the Universe's Messages

What you seek is seeking you.

— RUMI

Communication with the Divine isn't a one-way street—you talk, the Divine talks back. And the Divine's part of the conversation isn't always initiated by you. The universe talks to us in delightful ways every day. These communiqués may come in response to a petition, or they may simply be sent along to tell you something about your journey.

So how does the universe talk to us? Through signs and symbols that tell us we are on the right path. They're like God cheering us on—telling us we're going in the right direction, giving us hints about where to go next, and sometimes telling us we need to stop altogether and turn around. For example, a friend called me yesterday laughing. Out of a sense of guilt and obligation, she had said yes to a speaking engagement that she didn't really want to do—and she regretted it immediately. She called me in the middle of her drive to the venue. The trip, which usually takes just over an hour, took her three hours. There was flooding. And flashing road signs that said things like "Slow down. Don't drown" and "Do not travel any further. Flood watch. Extreme danger." She said she understood the signs loud and clear. She knew she would always remember this particular trip in the future when she's tempted to say yes when she really wants to say no.

The signs are everywhere—you just have to be open to seeing them. One morning while working on the first draft of this book, I was reading through Kyle Gray's book *Angel Prayers* for some inspiration before sitting down to write. My copy had just come in the mail the day before. I put it on my bedside table that night. The next morning, I opened it randomly to the page about Archangel Metatron. Here's what it says: "Metatron has a lot to do with our planet's changes and transitions. At the moment, he's helping us harness the new energies that are being offered to us by the universe. I call him 'the angel who connects heaven to Earth.'" A big smile came over my face—I understood the magic of this connection. First, I had *no* idea about Metatron's role in connecting heaven and earth. Clearly, Metatron was the perfect "sign" as I began writing this book, which is all about bringing heaven to earth—creating your own personal heaven in your current life. Henceforth, I thanked him every day for helping inspire me in the writing of this book! Several months later, I was doing my 13 Holy Nights ritual that I do at the end of every year starting on Christmas Eve and ending on January 6. On Christmas Eve, you meditate, pick oracle cards, and receive guidance for the entire following year. The angel I picked (from Kyle's Angel Card deck) as the overarching influence for 2016, the year this book was published, was Metatron. Of course.

Another incidence of the universe speaking to me happened just recently. I recorded two videos that had tiny bouncing light orbs in them, which I didn't see until I posted them. I was told by a number of my Instagram followers that these little orbs are fairies visiting me. You don't have to believe me on this. But check this kind of thing out for yourself. Many people find orbs appearing in their photos . . . signs of Divine energy we can't explain. When I was little, I made paper doll fairies and played with them in the lilac bushes. The fact that some kind of energy is now showing up in my life that sure seems ethereal and fairylike is confirmation that my nervous system is finally relaxing back to its natural state of loving consciousness.

This "coincidence" of seeing just the symbol I needed to see for inspiration—with both Metatron and the fairies—is just one of the concrete and practical ways that the Divine is always talking with you. God is right here for you. You don't have to spend decades as a "seeker" in order to get information from the Divine. You're already there. You just have to know how that communication works—and let the scales of disbelief fall from your eyes.

The issue that most people have with recognizing that the universe is talking to them is that our reductionistic culture in general and the kind of science we practice has made us doubt these things. What I'm talking about in this chapter tends to be called "magical thinking," even though our ability to communicate directly with one another telepathically—and with the intelligence of the universe—has been proved repeatedly. From what I've seen, the universe—and your Soul—will use any means possible to get through to you. Signs can be anything: license plates, road signs, songs on the radio, or even chosen signs like tarot cards. Here are some of my favorites and how I use them.

Dreams

The most direct, consistent, and powerful communication you will ever get from your Soul comes directly through dreams. Therefore, it's important for you to pay attention to and work consciously with your dreams. And like everything, this is a discipline that is well worth it.

Dreams contain inspiration, warnings, and prophesy about your future. In his book *The Toltec Secret: Dreaming Practices of the Ancient Mexicans*, Sergio Magaña, who comes from this 1,400-year-old lineage, points out that there are two different realities: the *naqual* (where dreams come from) and the *tonal* (waking life). He says that the naqual is four times more important than the tonal because everything that happens to us in waking life was first shown to us in a dream.

That doesn't mean that what you experience in a dream will inevitably come to pass in waking life. The main thing is to get the message so you can change the outcome when possible. You can even work to make this change in the naqual by reentering your dream and changing the ending. (See the box on the next page on how to do this.)

Magaña says that those who don't pay attention to their dreams are like the walking dead. I've come to see the wisdom of that statement.

Both Sigmund Freud and his student Carl Jung—both fathers of modern psychology—knew and wrote about the power of dreams as Soul communication. Those who train at the Jung Institute in Switzerland are trained extensively in dream analysis. Marion Woodman, the prolific writer and psychoanalyst, worked with and wrote about the astounding power of dream imagery to help and heal. Her books are classics.

One of my doctor friends told me about an experience he had that made him reconsider the power of dreams. He had a vivid dream that he was bleeding to death from his rectum. He went in for testing and, sure enough, they found a very small colon cancer. It was removed and he's been fine ever since. He credits the dream with saving his life. Dr. Larry Burk, a radiologist and the author of *Let Magic Happen,* has done extensive research on dreams and has published a study on dreams of breast cancer as a reliable diagnostic tool. Dreams can be so helpful and accurate; you have to wonder why the medical profession ignores them!

I began an in-depth study of my own dreams with clinical psychologist Doris E. Cohen, author of *Repetition: Past Lives, Life, and Rebirth,* back in 2012 when my ego was being shredded by the loss of a man I truly loved. Doris taught me that the subconscious mind is very efficient, and it will use whatever is currently going on in your life to make a point. That's likely to include imagery from a recently watched TV show or movie. That does *not* mean that the TV show caused you to dream what you're dreaming. Your subconscious is just using that character to make a point. For example, I dreamed about the character Jake on *Scandal* once.

What he represented was loyalty, integrity, and skill—the very things I like in a man. I was not dreaming about Jake, per se. I think one of the reasons celebrities are so adored in our society is because they enact roles for the entire collective and we project onto them. In this, they do our psyches a big service.

Without the dreams and my work with Doris as a lifeline, I might have slipped into despair and bitterness. Instead, I worked through my pain and wrote *Goddesses Never Age*—a title that was given to me by Doris during one of our dream work sessions. And this book has inspired and uplifted thousands of women all over the world. All because I followed the dictates of my own Soul—and was willing to transform my own pain.

How to Work with, Remember, and Interpret Your Dreams

1. Set your intention to remember your dreams. Just say out loud or to yourself something like "Divine Beloved, please help me to relax and remember my dreams tonight." Have a pen, paper, flashlight, or recording device right on your bedside table.

2. Ask a question that you would like to have answered in your dream. Ask that the imagery be easy to understand and interpret. Then let go of it all and drift into sleep.

3. If a dream awakens you in the middle of the night, it likely has an important message. So make sure you at least jot down a few details to remember it in the morning. In your sleepy state between the world of waking and sleeping, when the dream is *very* vivid, you'll be certain you could never forget the details. You will if you don't write down at least a few things about it. Trust me on this one. It's happened to me dozens of times.

4. As soon as you awaken, lie in bed for a moment, remembering the details of the dream before they slip away.

Write them down. I personally dictate them into my iPhone as voice memos. Later I write them up in Word documents and put them into monthly files that I keep on my computer.

5.   Give the dream a title—like a headline in a newspaper. This will encapsulate the wisdom in the dream and, in the future, will often bring the entire dream back to you in vivid detail.

6.   Check for recurrent themes in your dreams. And also any animals. I love it when animals show up in my dreams. They are always highly symbolic. I always look up the symbol the next day. *Animal Speak* by Ted Andrews is my favorite book for this. Also *Medicine Cards* by Jamie Sams and David Carson. You can also Google the name of the animal and the word *meaning*, e.g., "gorilla meaning."

7.   Other common and useful symbols and themes include clothing and shoes, which represent the roles you play in life. The hair on your head represents the thoughts in your head, so a new hair color or hairstyle indicates a new way of thinking. Cars represent the Self moving through life. Houses are also the Self—and the basement is the unconscious. When you find new rooms you didn't know were there, it means you are opening up to new aspects of your Self.

8.   Dr. Larry Burk suggests that you ask yourself, "What does the dream want?" Stop and listen for the first thought that comes into your head. Write it down. He says to seriously consider that the spirit world may have a question it wants you to answer in return.

9.   Share the dream with someone. Very often, recounting the dream out loud with a trusted friend or therapist will illuminate the meaning very quickly simply through the process of sharing.

Note how often you will remember a dream you had the night before—but much later in the day—like the afternoon. See if you can determine what jogged your memory enough to remember the dream then. Write it down. Don't dismiss it. Doris, my dream therapist, tells me that we usually dream the same kinds of things hundreds of times before we get the message. That is how compassionate our Souls are!

If a dream brings up an unresolved issue or bothers you in some way, you can, in waking life, simply close your eyes and reenter the dream. Change the ending. Remember—this is a free-will universe. We can change our future by changing our present. And whether the imagery comes in a dream or in a meditation, it's all coming from the same place.

Songs

As I already mentioned, I often hear songs when I am in the middle of Divine Love meditations—and they are always relevant. Music has a way of going right into our Souls, so hearing a particular song can often serve as an oracle. For example, in his iconoclastic memoir, *Not for Sale: Finding Center in the Land of Crazy Horse*, Kevin Hancock, the owner of Hancock Lumber here in Maine, writes about pulling out of the driveway at the home of his friend Rosie—a woman who lives on the Pine Ridge Indian Reservation in South Dakota. Kevin has been inexorably drawn there after an evolutionary astrology reading helped him make sense of losing his voice to a mysterious condition known as spasmodic dysphonia. Bringing together his distant past and his present, Kevin writes eloquently of the pull that has brought him out West. Again and again. To places he has never been but that are so familiar. Places where he feels at home. He writes, "As I pull down Rosie's winding gravel drive, the radio is tuned to 94.7 KCNB out of Chadron, Nebraska, where Phillip Phillips's hit song 'Home' begins to play. All about being lost and being found and finally feeling at home."

Yep—the Divine even comes with a soundtrack.

Kevin's journey to Pine Ridge and the surrounding area really was—on a Soul level—coming home. He was coming home to a deeper part of himself that had been missing in his daily life before this. And also returning to an important place in a past life. The signs and songs simply show the way—and act as trail markers along the journey. For all of us.

License Plates, Signs, Clocks

As I said earlier, the signs are everywhere. Even in some seriously unexpected places. My friend Tosha Silver, author of *Change Me Prayers*, shares delightful notes on social media and in her books and seminars about the messages that the Divine presents regularly. Often through license plates, road signs, or random objects on the sidewalk. Ever since learning about this kind of oracle—and seeing the hilarious pictures Tosha posts on Facebook—I've paid far more attention to these things in my own life. And I am often amused by the accuracy of the message from the car in front of me. For example, one day I was driving into Portland for a tango lesson and was feeling a little depressed. I had even considered canceling the lesson. When I saw that the car a bit ahead of me had the license plate FUN, it snapped me right back to my usual jovial self. It was as if the Divine looked at me and said, "Hey you. Dancing tango is just about the most fun you can have. So lighten up!"

Another one of my favorite signs came in late March last year when I saw something in my driveway that I thought was a piece of trash. When I went out to pick it up, it turned out to be a helium balloon floating just barely above the pavement. It had the words *Be My Valentine* on it. How in the world did that thing hang around and land in the middle of my driveway weeks after February 14? I have no idea, but it was the perfect sign for the year. I took a picture and texted it to Tosha. And at that very moment—all the way across the country in San Francisco—a guy ran past her with a T-shirt that said "My Muddy Valentine," a reference to an annual race through the mud during which people have actually met the loves of their lives. Both Tosha and I have been profoundly interested in finding true partnership in all areas of our lives—starting inside of ourselves. We both know that our culture's insistence on finding "completeness" via romantic love is fraught with peril until we find that completeness within ourselves. The valentine balloon and Muddy Valentine T-shirt, simultaneously showing up on both coasts, were Divine winks assuring both of us that we were right on track!

One of the regular signs I get from the Divine is when I look down at my phone and see that the time is a multiple of 11. Eleven is a spiritual mastery path number in numerology. It also signifies that the angels are near. Seeing 11:11 or 4:44 or 3:33 is like another wink from the Divine. Whatever I'm doing at the moment feels Divinely timed, and I know I'm right on track.

So the next time you look at your phone and it's a multiple of 11, smile, take a screenshot, and know that you are moving forward as you should be. Also note whatever you happen to be doing at the time. Are you going into a meeting? Just meeting someone new? Connect the sign with what is going on in your life at the moment.

This happened to me one day while I was writing this book, at exactly 4:44 P.M. I had to e-mail a friend to say that I was not going to be able to go on a trip where we had planned to meet up. I was worried about disappointing him, but that 4:44 timing was just the sign I needed to know that I was making the right decision. I sent the e-mail right away! He was indeed disappointed. Several weeks later, he broke his leg skiing, which meant that he wouldn't have been able to make the trip anyway. Divine guidance is a prospective process, meaning that it takes you forward into the future without telling you the reason. It can only be fully understood in retrospect, when you look back.

Oracle Cards, Tarot Readings, Psychics

Some of the most common places people go to find signs that they're on the right path are oracle cards, tarot readings, and psychics. These modes of communication are well known. I have about 20 different oracle card decks I keep right near my dining room. The current decks I use most are Colette Baron-Reid's *Wisdom of the Oracle Divination Cards*, Doreen Virtue's *Goddess Guidance Oracle Cards*, Jamie Sams and David Carson's *Medicine Cards*, and Kyle Gray's *Angel Prayers Oracle Cards*. I often pick a card for guidance on a particular topic. Or I do a relationship reading in which I pick one card for me, one card for the issue (or other person), and a third card to put in between them to get a sense of what the situation is about.

When you are looking for simple guidance using an oracle deck, you ask the question you need answered, then shuffle the deck and pick a card. This card will help you see what you need to see about the situation your question focused on. To help you understand the meaning of the card, most oracle decks come with a guidebook that provides an extended explanation of what the card means.

Aside from my oracle cards, I keep a small travel deck of tarot cards in my purse at all times. Over the years, I have found it infinitely practical to pull cards to help me make decisions on everything from which restaurant to order from to whether to say yes or no to an offer. For a simple yes-or-no question, I work with the tarot deck and two small pieces of paper that I carry along with it. One says YES and one says NO. I keep the yes and no notes folded so that I don't know which is which. To help me make my yes-or-no decision, I put these folded pieces of paper on the table, connect with the Divine, and then pull a tarot card for each of them. Once the cards are drawn, I unfold the yes and no papers and look at the card associated with each. I know the tarot symbolism well enough to get added insight into my decisions. There are always nuances of meaning and guidance that are very helpful.

If the question I have can't be answered with a simple yes or no—if there are a series of options—I still follow a similar process. I write each option down on a small piece of paper, fold the papers, and then, after connecting with the Divine, put a card down faceup on each piece of paper. This gives me in-depth information about a choice that would otherwise have evaded my intellect and ego. I also often do a particular spread as a kind of "weather report" to see where I am. If there is something about my thinking that's off, it is nearly always reflected in the cards. In the box on page 56, I outline the process I use when I need guidance in decision making.

Tarot decks come in many forms—from the Rider-Waite-Smith deck, which is one of the most commonly used, to my favorite, the Motherpeace Round Tarot Deck. The biggest difference in most decks is the illustrations, which generally have a theme, such as nature. The cards of the tarot are split into two categories: Major Arcana and Minor Arcana. The Minor Arcana are Wands, Swords, Cups, and Circles (Discs or Pentacles), and these cards are numbered or contain court imagery, like the Jack, Queen, and King in a standard deck of playing cards. Generally there are 56 Minor Arcana cards, though this does vary based on the deck you get. The Major Arcana cards, of which there are 22, are numbered either 1 to 22 or 0 to 21. They are also named with ideas such as Wheel of Fortune, Death, the Devil, the Magician, the Sun, and so on. These cards represent larger cosmic principles.

Each card in a tarot deck has a meaning, and in a reading, the Minor Arcana cards relay subtlety and detail about situations. These are the "little" cards that speak to the personal pieces of a reading. The Major Arcana cards indicate something of greater significance; they express universal ideas and archetypes.

I can't teach you how to do a full reading in this book—because, like reading an astrological chart, tarot reading is an art. Luckily most decks come with information on how to do a reading, along with information on the meaning of each card. I suggest you get a deck and start to familiarize yourself with the cards and the process. It's also helpful to get a reading from a skilled card reader.

Decision-Making Help from a Tarot Deck

There are many ways to get information from the use of tarot cards, and while I can't go into it fully in this book, here's one of my favorite simple ways to get some guidance.

1. **Understand your problem:** While I was writing this book, I was trying to decide whether or not to use boxes (like this one). There are pros and cons to boxes—they set off material nicely so it's easy to find, but they do break up the narrative of a chapter, which changes the character. I was leaning toward boxes, but I wasn't sure they were right for this book.

2. **Get clear on the options available:** For me, my options were boxes or no boxes. While this example is pretty basic, there can be any number of options depending on the decision you face.

3. **Write out the options:** I put "boxes" and "no boxes" on separate little pieces of paper and folded them up so I didn't know which was which.

4. **Ask your question:** I asked, "Which of these options is the best solution?"

5. **Lay out your cards:** For each of the options you wrote down, lay one card on top. I got the Devil card for "no boxes." Clear message. The Devil isn't necessarily bad; it just represents being disconnected from one's Divinity. Obviously I went with boxes.

While it may seem confusing to use tarot cards in this way since each card has a different meaning, I have found that it's gotten easier to interpret the cards over the years. Over time you get really good at this. And once you know your deck, the deck speaks to you. And you get far more information than just the face value of the card itself. Remember, tarot cards arise from deeply archetypal patterns of human consciousness that have been passed down through the ages.

One thing to remember as you're working with tarot cards: The cards have no power in and of themselves. I often find that, just like with astrology, people are afraid of getting a "bad" reading. But this stems from the misuse of intuitive powers for personal gain that has too often been associated with all things psychic. Just for fun, I sometimes go to the kinds of psychics who have neon signs in their offices, highly visible from the street, and I've rarely found them very helpful. The readings they give can be either disempowering and completely void of hope or overly optimistic. This does nothing but create bad energy, and since most of us go to psychics when our egos desperately want something to be true (a job, a lover, a move), we need some reassurance. Readings *can* be really helpful from the right people.

Remember—just because someone is psychic and can see other realms doesn't mean that what they're getting from that realm is helpful, accurate, or even anything you should be involved in. Like I say to people who know how to connect with the dead, "Just because they're dead doesn't mean they're enlightened." Just because someone is psychic or has intuitive abilities doesn't make them healing forces. Sometimes they have unclean energy and use their gifts to exploit others. So-called supernatural powers are available to anyone who cares to learn them. So don't get caught up with those who use them to gain power. Being a force of light and healing is quite another matter. The most spiritual thing to do in any circumstance is to give others the benefit of the doubt, be kind, gracious, and forgiving. Even when it's inconvenient.

So when I do a reading for someone else (or even myself) and get some problematic cards—like the Devil or one of the suit of Swords—I just point out that the card is simply the result of how they are thinking about an issue in the moment. A while later I'll redo the cards to show them how a change in thinking changed the reading. Bingo! They take their power back. And the cards become what they are: simply a tool to figure out what you're really thinking or feeling so you can change it up for the better!

Divinely Orchestrated Synchronicities

One of my absolute favorite forms of communication from the Divine is synchronicity—events that seem to happen "by chance" but are so fraught with meaning that you can't possibly believe they are random. Synchronicities are orchestrated all the time by a mysterious force that our egos simply cannot comprehend. This is part of the magic.

I experienced the most amazing Divinely orchestrated series of events in the late summer of 2015. It was truly stunning. Before I tell you about that, however, let me set up its significance by taking you back to 2012, when I fulfilled a longtime dream of going to Buenos Aires to dance tango. While the trip had some wonderful moments, overall it wasn't what I dreamed it would be.

On my second day there I was happily walking down a sunny, crowded street with a fellow tango dancer, a friend who had visited the city many times and was fluent in Spanish—and who had told me how safe it was. Out of the blue, a man came up behind me, put his hands around my neck, and snatched my necklace. It all happened very fast and it left me shaken and terrified, with a scratched and bruised neck. That moment set the tone for my three-week adventure. That thief didn't just steal any old necklace. This one was not only expensive; it was a Goddess necklace—gold in the shape of a crescent moon. It had been a collective birthday gift from a group of close friends, and it was, hands down, my favorite piece of jewelry—a signature piece that I wore all the time.

When this happened, I wrote about it on Facebook to get support. Tosha Silver, who I barely knew at that time, sent me a most meaningful message saying that many times the Goddess herself demands a sacrifice as part of our healing. Perhaps this particular omen was a really good one.

Though I miss that necklace to this day, and though I've suggested to the universe a few things I would like to see happen to that thief, I also knew that the theft was highly symbolic.

Part of my life's journey has been to learn and make peace with the fact that my true soul mate is not outside of me. It's inside. No attempt to make it anyone else would ever work long term. (Trust me—I've tried every other avenue. Including online dating. You name it. I've done it.) This doesn't mean that I wouldn't prefer a relationship. It's just that this inner work has had to be done. It's the inner marriage for which I was born.

At the time I went to Argentina, I hadn't yet accepted this part of my journey. I was grieving the loss of a relationship that I thought was going to be "the one." I truly believed that he was the one who would complete me. But the truth is that we all have masculine and feminine energies within us, and if we are to live happily, these need to be balanced within us. No external force will ever make us complete. It's one thing to know this intellectually—I always have known it. It's quite another to be put to the test by losing the one you see as the love of your life. The theft of my necklace brought home my need to set outside love aside and focus on balancing my masculine and feminine energies.

Between 2012 and my trip in 2015, I worked relentlessly on this goal of balance. Frankly, anything else was just too painful. And since I don't use drugs or alcohol, I wasn't even numbing the pain; I was just feeling yearning and despair that wouldn't go away, no matter what I did. Then in the spring of 2015, a good friend invited me on a special, invitation-only trip to a sacred site that had always fascinated her. Many of my colleagues were also going. Everything about this trip—from the planning to each stop along the way—acted as a nod from the Divine, acknowledging that my work was going well. I was on the right path.

The synchronicity of the trip began in the planning phase, with discussions of travel starting when the planets Mars (masculine) and Venus (feminine) were doing a most unusual dance in the sky—they were coming together three separate times, which is quite rare. The trip itself, which also happened during the Mars-Venus dance, was a retreat to Mount Shasta, which is said to be a special power spot on planet Earth. You can feel the high vibration and purity of the place. And you can't get a cell signal most of the time either.

While there I stayed at a place called Stewart Springs, which, among other things, features special tubs for soaking in mineral-rich spring waters. I learned that Stewart Springs has both a male and female spring that come out of the ground at the same place. The female spring leaves a red residue from the iron in it, while the male spring leaves a white residue from calcite. It is the male spring water that is used in the baths and in the plunge pool for after the sauna. Apparently the female spring water "eats" the pipes and can't be used.

At the place where the two springs emerge from the earth, there is a gazebo with a clear dome so you can look down to observe them. The open-air gazebo also has a large altar where people have left notes, crystals, pictures, and various sacred objects as a kind of homage to this most special place—and the energies of masculine and feminine that arise side by side from inside the earth.

I loved being at this gazebo and left an offering, along with a prayer and an intention to merge the male and female energies within myself. And once again, for about the thousandth time, I surrendered to the Divine my yearning for a man to complete me. It felt so Divinely orchestrated to be at this particular place on the planet at this particular time.

Interestingly, while I was at Mount Shasta, I learned that there is only one other place on Earth where male and female springs arise at the same place: Glastonbury, England, a place I was scheduled to visit one month later during another Mars-Venus meeting. I was gobsmacked. What were the chances? Nil. Divine guidance had orchestrated a most profound pilgrimage for me to the only two sacred sites where the masculine and feminine energies come out of the earth, at the very same time that these energies were dancing in the sky above.

While at Glastonbury, I visited the male White Spring, which is covered by a gothic stone structure—complete with pools and altars to both the Goddess and to the Horned God. Venus and Mars, if you will. We sang a song to the Goddess. I left offerings for both the male and female aspects of Divinity. And then we visited the female Chalice Well, with its beautiful depictions of the Vesica Piscis in the walkway leading to it and in the covering of the well itself. The Vesica Piscis is made up of two intersecting circles symbolizing the union of Spirit and Matter, or masculine and feminine. I filled bottles with Chalice Well water to bring home and bathed some crystals in the spring water.

The trips to Mount Shasta and Glastonbury were transformational for me. They reinforced the importance of owning my own value and my own power. And they provided me an opportunity to take stock of how very far I had come since the Goddess reclaimed *her* necklace in Buenos Aires.

The good news is that that yearning and heartbreak are now a thing of the past. I'm happier and more fulfilled than I have ever been—a huge vibration upgrade. It feels like something I've been working on for a zillion lifetimes—and I finally "got it."

Magic Is Everywhere

During my trip to Glastonbury, I decided to visit St. Margaret's Chapel, a part of the huge Glastonbury Abbey area. I wanted to do this because back in the day, I did my obstetrical training at the former St. Margaret's Hospital for Women on the top of Dorchester Hill in Boston. St. Margaret of Scotland, who is associated with the Divine Feminine, spent her life in service, loving everyone unconditionally. Each day at St. Margaret's Hospital began with Sister Anna reading morning prayers over the loud speaker—prayers that could be heard throughout the hospital even as we performed a difficult delivery or a C-section. Even when we were resuscitating a baby. I always felt comforted by those prayers.

There was also a plaque at the scrub sink that I'd read before going into surgery. It was a prayer to Archangel Raphael, the great healer. Though I don't remember the words, the gist of it was that we prayed that Archangel Raphael would work through us while we operated so that we could be a force for healing. I loved knowing that I wasn't alone in the operating room—that forces *greater* than me were helping. As I sat in St. Margaret's Chapel in Glastonbury, I lit a candle and made an offering to her. Thanking her for all that she had done while here in a body—and all that she continues to do in Spirit.

Back when I was learning surgery at St. Margaret's, I had to master surgical skills, and anatomy, and knot tying. No matter what you find yourself doing, there is no shortcut to mastering your trade or profession through work and discipline and time spent. That's a given. But when you also invite in the Big Magic, you soon realize that there are forces much greater than your own intellect that you can call on to assist you with all aspects of your life. And that everything from license plates to chance meetings will show up to keep you on track. Nothing is more exhilarating.

CHAPTER 5

Thoughts and Feelings: The Basic Building Blocks of Your Reality

Thoughts become things . . . choose the good ones.

— MIKE DOOLEY

Let's now move away from Spirit and into the power of your mind to make life easy. The first thing you have to understand in the realm of the mind is that the quality of your life is created by the quality of the thoughts you habitually think. Thoughts are powerful electromagnetic events in the brain that create a vortex of energy both around you as well as inside you. As you think, so you feel, and as you feel, so you vibrate. As you vibrate, so you attract. Positive thoughts have a high vibration, and negative thoughts have a low vibration. Every single thought you think is also accompanied by subtle changes in your immune, endocrine, and central nervous systems.

Positive thoughts are accompanied by positive changes in your body's biochemistry. Negative thoughts, on the other hand, tend to depress both your immunity and your mood. And remember that both types of thoughts tend to attract their physical equivalents. That is why getting a handle on the quality of your daily thoughts—and choosing them more deliberately and consciously—is a powerful tool for making your life easy.

Sounds simple, doesn't it? And it actually is simple. The problem is this: It is estimated that we think about 60,000 thoughts per day. Of these, 80 percent are negative and habitual, e.g., "It's too late for me to [blank]." Or "My father was right. I'll never amount to anything." And on it goes. Thoughts, like genes, are handed down in families and tribes, and they are highly contagious. For example, if you are brought up in a family that believes rich people are evil, chances are very good that you will have exactly the same thought. Thinking differently from your tribe is a considered a betrayal. And, as you will remember from an earlier chapter, tribes punish what they consider betrayal with shame and abandonment. Because shame and abandonment are painful, most people don't want to risk changing their habitual thoughts, lest they no longer fit in. I'm bringing this up now so that, when you meet the inevitable resistance that arises with changing thoughts, you'll know you're on the right track!

Luckily, we all have the ability to change the way we think. In his magnificent TED talk, Dr. Joe Dispenza goes into great detail about how thoughts and their accompanying feelings actually change the neuronal patterns in our brains. Repetitive thoughts and feelings of joy or compassion actually create new connections in the brain, and the old ones—of depression and sadness—eventually fall away. But only with repetition and dedication. What we've learned about the brain is that it gets good at whatever it does the most. Repetitive thoughts create faster and larger neural pathways in the brain much the same way as nature trails in the woods become easier to follow and walk on the more people walk on them. As the popular axiom goes, "Neurons that fire together, wire together." The ability of the brain to change its wiring with different thought and movement patterns is known as neuroplasticity. And that quality stays with us for a lifetime, which means that it's never too late to change your thought patterns and thus improve your life.

Changing your thoughts takes repetition, self-love, optimism, patience, and discipline. When you begin to pay loving attention to your thoughts—no matter how negative they are—you will gradually upgrade to more positive ones quite naturally. The end result will be that your life is forever changed for the better. Your thoughts and the associated chemicals that affect your body will all be working for you. So let's get started with some tried-and-true ways to change your thoughts.

Loving Your Inner Innocence

Spiritual teacher Matt Kahn points out that what we call "the shadow" is really our inner child and inner innocence that has been ignored and shamed for so long it will do anything to get our attention. To emphasize this point, in one of his lectures on YouTube, he recounted a time in his life when the power of his inner child became obvious. He was communing with ascended masters and other high-vibration spiritual guides when a voice in his head said, "Go f**k yourself." It was the voice of his inner child, whose needs he had been ignoring. It turns out that the inner child loves four-letter words for emphasis.

When I heard this, a lightbulb went on for me. Of course! Almost every single one of us, including me, tends to have a deep-seated belief from our past that what we have to say or contribute is not good enough. This belief comes from the overstimulated nervous system—and subsequent unconscious beliefs—of our inner child. And the inner children of our parents, and their parents, and so on.

You will not be successful at changing your thoughts sustainably, let alone your behavior, until you have loved this part of yourself. You must love it as you would a five-year-old in pain. So while you're catching yourself thinking negative thoughts, first say something like "I love you. You're beautiful. I value you. I forgive you. You are precious" to the child inside who is just letting you know how she feels. Put your hand over your heart and say these words out loud. Like you mean it. Because just putting an intellectual layer of "choose the thought that feels better" on top of the pain of your inner child is not going to work. She needs your love, and she's going to keep demanding it until you pay attention. So start by understanding that those negative thoughts are simply coming from the aspect of yourself that needs love. Attend to this part first, and then watch how easily you can change your thoughts.

Limit Exposure to Negativity

Aside from loving your inner child, there are quite a number of things you can do to help you change your thoughts. The first is to limit negative outside influences. This includes much of mainstream media, music, video games, and the Internet, along with anyone who drains your energy. Remember that our entire culture is set up to feed our egos and keep us afraid. We're constantly being bombarded with things that keep us stuck in fear and negativity. Anything that elicits fear, anger, fatigue, or a sense of powerlessness needs to be cut out of your life—or at least reduced as much as possible.

Let's take mainstream news, for example. It's fine to stay informed about the world. And quite frankly, you'd have to be living under a rock not to be informed these days given the 24/7 news cycle and the Internet. But just be media savvy and know your sources. Mainstream news chooses the most extreme situations from all over the globe—then adds powerful, evocative music and replays scenes of pain, anger, and mayhem repeatedly 24/7. Mainstream news is a business that is supported by advertisers who have a particular point of view. Most commercial television shows, for example, are supported by Big Food and Big Pharma, and the content of the shows they support is generally in alignment with the message they want you to believe. If you are media savvy and know how mass media works, then fine. You won't be unconsciously imbibing the negativity.

But I, for one, am rarely able to maintain my usually optimistic cheery mood after I've watched the evening news. So I don't watch it. Why? Because no human being has nervous, endocrine, and immune systems that were designed to process the negative news from all over the planet that's being piped into their living room on a daily basis. Frankly, most of us have enough on our plates with frustrations from our own jobs, neighborhoods, and families, let alone the entire planet.

The reason why it's so important to avoid negativity is because it disconnects you from your power to make a positive change in the world and in your life. It does just the opposite. It deadens us and renders us powerless. How can we possibly make a difference in the face of so much pain and destruction? It's paralyzing to stay in this low-vibration state. So you must do whatever it takes to raise your vibration to a higher level characterized by optimism, hope, and joy.

When you are connected to the Divine part of yourself, you are aligned with the power of pure positive energy. And that pure positive energy creates a magnetic field that draws in more pure positive energy. This is the kind of energy that thrives on inspiration and the lifting up of others. It builds things up, rather than tearing them down. It is the exact opposite of the energy that produces vandalism and rampages of violence. Aligning with pure, positive energy inspires you to take a walk in nature, smile at strangers, and become a force for good. And that pure, positive energy is what uplifts and heals the planet. Powerfully so. And that is scientific fact.

The Power of Affirmations

Chances are that you've heard of using affirmations as a way to change ingrained negative thought patterns. But what exactly are affirmations, and how do you use them?

Affirm means to state as a fact—strongly and publicly—and/or to support emotionally. Thus an affirmation is a strong statement spoken or written as fact that supports you emotionally in order to bring forth or emphasize something you desire. An example of an affirmation is "I am free, happy, and healthy. Happiness is my birthright. I was born to be joyous."

To use affirmations, you simply say them. Look in the mirror and speak them aloud. When you do this, you are literally creating new neural pathways in your brain. It doesn't happen right away, but remember what I said at the beginning of this chapter: Your brain gets good at what it does often. So give yourself time and also make sure that the very act of affirming something is enjoyable. Affirmations that are done as a chore and without your wholehearted attention won't create much change in your life.

What Goes into an Affirmation?

Affirmations are strong statements, set in the present tense, that express some desired outcome in your life. For example, "Life supports me in every way." Or "I am healthy and completely pain free." Pretty simple, right?

There are, however, a couple of traps you can set for yourself when coming up with affirmations. It's important not to sabotage yourself with an affirmation that's a real long shot for you. An example would be, "I happily make $1,000,000 per year, tax free" when you are saddled with debt and are working for a relativity low wage. It's too much of a jump for your brain to handle that new prosperous reality. And your body and mind are likely to rebel.

Also keep in mind that you don't want to make the affirmations too detailed or specific, such as "The love of my life, who has a great job, makes a lot of money, has a wonderful relationship with his family, and is compassionate to all beings, is already here." Tosha Silver calls this "giving God a shopping list"—a great term. But it's much more effective to make a broad, general statement about how you want to feel: "The love of my life, who makes me feel happy and alive, is already here." When we give God our "shopping list" of specific things we want, it limits what the Divine can do through us. And trust me, we want the Divine part of ourselves to lead us, because the Divine knows what we need better than our limited intellects ever could.

> Remember that affirmations don't actually make things happen. Instead, they can raise your vibration so that you are more receptive to the desired outcome.

I have always been interested in the link between our thoughts, our health, and our circumstances. I kept *Heal Your Body*, Louise Hay's classic little blue book on the mental causes of physical illness, in my desk drawer at the office during my very first years in practice. I would get it out regularly to learn how to connect the dots between what people were experiencing in their bodies and what their thought patterns were. I saw that the mental patterns of thought and the physical manifestations of those thoughts matched up very well.

Though I always understood how thoughts work when it comes to health, my real test on the power of thoughts to change reality came around the subject of money. When I was going through my divorce, I was terrified that I'd lose my house and not be able to put my daughters through college. Like so many women, I had left the finances to my husband, sure that he knew much more about that boring subject than I did. But now I was in crisis. I had no other choice if I wanted to maintain any semblance of stability for myself and my children. The first thing I did was read *Think and Grow Rich* by Napoleon Hill, a classic published in 1937 about the connection between our thoughts and our income. I read this book and did every exercise like my life depended on it. At the same time, I read Catherine Ponder's *The Dynamic Laws of Prosperity*. Another classic.

I wanted to develop the kind of mind-set that would attract abundance. And I had to do this fast. Besides reading the books, I created some pro-prosperity affirmations. These weren't simply about money—though some were. They were about prosperity in all aspects of my life. They were about how I wanted to feel. How I wanted to live. How I wanted to interact with the world. These were some of my favorites:

- I am now experiencing perfect health, abundant prosperity, and complete and utter happiness. This is true because the world is full of charming people who now lovingly help me in every way.

- I am now come into an innumerable company of angels.

- I am now living a delightful, interesting, and satisfying life of the most widely useful kind.

- Because of my own increased wealth, health, and happiness, I am now able to help others live a delightful, interesting, and satisfying life of the most widely useful kind. My good—our good—is universal.

- Today I am reborn spiritually. I completely detach myself from my old way of thinking, and I bring Divine Love, light, health, joy, wealth, success, pleasure, prosperity, and abundance into my experience in concrete, definite ways.

- I soar above all problems and obstacles as I triumphantly move forward to claim my Divine birthright of unlimited wealth, health, love, prosperity, and abundance.

- I accept only harmony, peace of mind, radiantly good health, personal love, and overflowing financial abundance as the natural conditions in my daily life.

- There is great power in my joy, pleasure, and vision of a delightful life.

I said these affirmations out loud—every day, over and over again—while walking fast on a treadmill. I wanted the words to get into my body, so I said them with great enthusiasm to boost my vibration as high as I could get it. These statements helped make me into a far more solid container for abundance than I had been before. Little by little, day by day, they gave me the energy and inspiration I needed to do the nuts and bolts of becoming financially literate.

The power of affirmations in my own life is indisputable. I suggest that you create some of your own to help you shift in whatever way you need to shift. And add new ones regularly. Start each morning with a few. And put them on your bathroom mirror. If you'd like, you can sign up for daily affirmations delivered to your in-box right on my website (www.drnorthrup.com).

Proprioceptive Writing: Writing the Mind Alive

Proprioceptive writing is another powerful way to change your thoughts. I'll never forget the day I first heard about it, years ago. I was sitting in Labor and Delivery at the hospital and I saw a postcard for a workshop about something called proprioceptive writing. I knew about the proprioceptors in muscles that allow us to know—even with our eyes closed—where our arms and legs are in space. But I had no idea how this could apply to writing.

At the time I was actually having a problem with writing, which is probably why the postcard got my attention. Basically, I found it extremely taxing to write anything scientific. There was always a big, bad editor in my head telling me that I didn't know what I was doing. That I was wrong. And that I was unworthy. All my years of academic training and medical school had made the voice of self-doubt worse, not better.

So I contacted Linda Trichter Metcalf, the person who was leading the workshop, and asked her if this course might help me. Linda, who at the time also taught English at Pratt Institute in Brooklyn, New York, told me that her method worked well for anyone who wanted to get better at expressing themselves through writing—even medical writing. And so, pregnant with my second child, I signed up for a weekend workshop. And it changed my life. It helped me clear the mangrove swamp of my conditioned thoughts and beliefs so effectively that I eventually found my own unique writer's voice. The real me. It helped me understand what I really thought and believed—separate from the voice of my parents, my profession, my siblings, and my husband. It also allowed me to write my first book—and, quite frankly, all the subsequent books.

Proprioceptive writing, which helps you drill down to your base beliefs, was a lifeline that connected me to my Self. To my Soul. This method works because it helps you identify what you really believe about a subject by writing your thoughts and reflecting on them with empathy and compassion. You can do this on any topic. So for example, if you write about the word *mother*, proprioceptive writing will help you see what your mind has to say about that word. You will find yourself remembering all kinds of things about your mother that you didn't realize you remembered. As you write, you get very clear about what you really think—not just what you've been conditioned to think. Not just what you are supposed to think. And when you identify your true beliefs, without judging them, you can begin to change them. As Linda says on her website:

> Proprioceptive Writing is an important adjunct to the healing arts. Through Proprioceptive Writing people learn to express their thoughts without judging themselves, reflect on feelings without guilt or shame, and experience their emotions without being overwhelmed by them—the first step to emotional health.

Proprioceptive writing combines intellect, imagination, and intuition—all simultaneously. And it is done as a ritual. It's often done to Baroque music (Mozart, Bach, Vivaldi, and so on) because this music has been shown to entrain our creativity very effectively. You can also use Indian ragas, which elicit a different experience.

As you do this work, here's what you'll discover: Your thoughts have meaning. They have order. And they are going toward resolution and healing. This is so very reassuring for those of us who have been "schooled" out of our own unique genius. As Linda says, "The desire for the self, the desire not to live a life that doesn't feel like it's yours—that's why somebody might be attracted to this work."

How to Do a Write

The process of proprioceptive writing is pretty simple. You simply choose a topic and write while paying attention to your feelings and not judging what comes up. Here's a step-by-step overview, just to make things as easy as possible.

1. Gather the following supplies: a pen, a candle, matches, single sheets of 8½" x 11" white paper, a Baroque playlist that lasts for about 20 minutes. Baroque music has a very specific vibration that supports brain functioning; it's known as the Mozart effect. But you can experiment with other genres if you wish.

2. Lay out a stack of paper—20 sheets or so—and date the first page on the upper right-hand side. You will also number each page as you write, but only on one side, as you will only be writing on one side.

   - Once your paper is ready, start the music and light the candle.

   - Take a deep breath, and come up writing.

   - When you get to the end of the 20 minutes, finish up your current thought.

   - Then ask the following questions: "How do I feel now?" and "What story am I telling?"

   - Answer in writing. And take as long as you like or have time for. Usually you can do this in one to three lines.

   - Now—read your "write" out loud.

Remember: When you're writing, listen to the voice in your head—the witness self. Record what you hear. You are just a secretary. That's all. Write everything down that comes up, even if it sounds meaningless. Every thought has meaning and significance.

> Also listen for any word that has a "charge," and when the charged word arises (like *worthy* or *disappointed*), drill down on it by asking the proprioceptive question: "What do I mean by [blank]?" Then write down what you hear. Remember, you are just a secretary—writing down the thoughts in your mind.

Proprioceptive writing is powerful when you do it yourself, but there is a way to increase its effects even more. I believe that there is nothing more meaningful or holy or healing that doing proprioceptive writing as a group. Or at least with one other trusted person.

After the writing process, you can read your writes out loud. Then people can respond to your write by writing down what moved them or stood out for them. This allows us to hear ourselves reflected back to us by another. It's extraordinarily validating and strengthening as we learn how to trust our thoughts—and change them to more positively reflect the Divine within us. I've done this countless times with friends and family, and it never fails to bring us all closer. And also to reflect our true selves back to each other. Most people are amazed by what happens when they're given permission to free their minds and lose the editor who has been telling them they're doing everything wrong.

Meditation

Meditation of all different kinds has been shown to enhance physical health, lower blood pressure, lift depression, decrease acts of violence, and contribute to more well-being and happiness. By quieting thoughts through meditation, we quite naturally bounce back to the higher vibration we had as babies—before our egos were formed from chronic tension in our nervous systems. Herbert Benson, M.D., of Harvard was a pioneer in the study of meditation and coined the term *relaxation response* to describe what happens in our physical, emotional, and mental bodies during meditation. This response is what's responsible for the many benefits that meditators experience.

One of the nice things about meditation is that there are so many kinds. Walking meditation, where you simply move slowly while paying attention to all the sensations of your movement. Sitting meditation, where you focus on a mantra or on your breath. Mindfulness meditation, where you focus on the present moment in any situation, nonjudgmentally accepting any thoughts and sensations that come up. These are just some of the variations, and with so many options you can definitely find the type of meditation that appeals to you.

I learned Transcendental Meditation way back in the day. I even studied with the late Maharishi Mahesh Yogi, the founder of this technique. I practiced this meditation religiously for many years and learned to calm my mind and body quite effectively, but you don't have to do any formal studying to benefit from meditation. It can be as easy as simply closing your eyes and paying attention to your breathing.

Simple Meditations

Breathing Meditation: Breathing meditation is one of the simplest types of meditation you can do. Here's what you do: Sit comfortably. Set a timer for 15 minutes. Close your eyes. Breathe in for a count of four. Hold it for a moment. Then breathe out for a count of four.

Do this until your timer goes off. Heck, if you don't want to set a timer, just do it for a while. You'll notice that you become quite calm. And your vibration rises.

Realization Process: I recently worked with a type of meditation called the Realization Process. Created by Judith Blackstone, this process involves bringing your consciousness itself right into your tissues, starting with your feet. Try this: Close your eyes. Breathe in for a count of two and then breathe out for a count of two until your breathing is nice and smooth. Then put your consciousness right down in your feet. Relax your arches.

> Feel what it's like to be in your feet. Completely. Then move up your body slowly, staying in your feet but adding your legs. Then your knees. Then your hips. Then your pelvis. Then your torso. Your chest. Your neck. And finally up into the center of your head. Spend time in each area. Just being in it.

As you can see, meditation comes in all sorts of guises. It doesn't matter which one you work with, as the focus of every type is about bringing you into the present moment. Helping you see and accept your thoughts. Quieting your mind. And adding to your sense of peace and calm. Over time, as you practice meditation, it changes the holding patterns in your mind and body.

Self-Healing, Global Healing

By healing our thoughts, we are doing much more than simply fixing our own lives. Spiritual teacher and healer Matt Kahn points out that every time we meet our own anger, disappointment, or sadness with love, we change the world. There have been 60-plus studies published in peer-reviewed journals such as the *Journal of Conflict Resolution* showing that when just one percent of the population changes their habitual thought quality through practices like Transcendental Meditation, there is a measurable decrease in violent crime, robberies, and reported distress of all kinds.

The Global Coherence Initiative of the HeartMath Institute is also doing ongoing collaborative research involving sensors placed at various locations around the planet that actually measure the subtle electromagnetic field of the earth. Believe it or not, collective human emotions and thoughts have been found to affect the earth's magnetic field as measured through these sensors. When large numbers of people create heart-centered states of loving care and compassion, it results in a more coherent electromagnetic field around the earth that benefits everyone—plants, animals, and the planet itself. This is because there is a feedback loop between human beings and the earth's energetic/magnetic systems.

Every single person affects this global field because we are all interconnected with and affected by the magnetic fields generated by the sun and the earth. And every cell in our bodies is bathed in both an external and internal environment of fluctuating invisible magnetic forces.

The research on meditation and the Global Coherence Initiative are perfect examples of something Albert Einstein said back in 1946 after the first atomic bomb was dropped on Japan and the potential for global annihilation was a distinct possibility: "A new type of thinking is essential if mankind is to survive and move to higher levels." Knowing that the quality of our thoughts and emotions really matters—to everyone—is truly a new type of thinking!

Whatever Arises: Love That

In *Whatever Arises, Love That*, Matt Kahn suggests that when a painful thought or circumstance presents itself, we simply say, "Thank you," which is an act of faith in itself because our ego tends to judge everything as either bad or good. But when you say thank you, you're acknowledging that there is a greater wisdom at play that your ego can't identify. Kahn also suggests that we say "I love you" to ourselves. And mean it. Because that thought and the negativity associated with it arise from the lack of love—and the lack of connection with our Source. But there's more. These unpleasant thoughts and emotions are actually discharging negativity not only from *your* life but also from the lives of everyone else. As you feel it, you heal it. For everyone. And so when you have those negative thoughts, you need more love, not less. Your power lies in catching yourself in the middle of your anger, sadness, or frustration, and then realizing that these represent opportunities to thank and love yourself, not judge yourself. You have the power to say, "I love you, right there. Right there in the thick of it." When you do this, the angry, disconnected part of yourself dissolves because its message gets heard. It gets the attention and love it has always been needing.

When we stop fighting with ourselves, when we no longer beat ourselves up as unworthy or flawed, when we align with the Divine and love ourselves, we are contributing to higher vibrations for everyone. And given the connection between your thoughts, emotions, and the planet herself, you might very well be contributing to rain in areas that have experienced drought. Or helping a woman conceive a much-wanted child. Or making it more likely that bees will find flowers to pollinate. Yes, your thoughts and emotions—when connected with the Divine—really are capable of doing all that and more.

CHAPTER 6

The Power of Giving and Receiving

Until we can receive with an open heart, we are never really giving with an open heart. When we attach judgment to receiving help, we knowingly or unknowingly attach judgment to giving help.

— BRENÉ BROWN

I'm sure you've heard the old adage that it is more blessed to give than to receive, right? And while it certainly feels good to give, there is no joy in the giving unless there is a gracious receiver on the other end. Both giving and receiving, if done with love and joy and openness, can act as a salve to soothe a tired soul. So if you want your life to really flow and be easy, it's best to learn how to do both graciously and happily.

Most of us have had our receiving wings clipped at an early age, especially women. And we've been conditioned to go overboard in the giving department. We need balance here because without it, we are constantly stressed and drained.

Let's just take the holiday season as an example. Holiday gift giving has become such a burden that we quite naturally associate the holidays with stress. This is ridiculous. The time from Thanksgiving through New Year's should be characterized by taking stock of the past year and enjoying the real meaning of the holidays. Instead it has become an "Are you ready for Christmas?" frenzy. When I was working at the hospital, I used to have recurrent nightmares about having to go up to a store that's open 24/7 to get my daughters their Christmas gifts on Christmas Eve. During those days I over-gave gifts at Christmas because I felt guilty about spending so much time at work. Not exactly a balance between giving and receiving.

Now that we're all adults, we've consciously curtailed obligatory holiday gift giving to relieve stress. And the relief is palpable. We focus on getting together, preparing meals, enjoying each other's company, and choosing one gift for a Yankee swap. Always fun. It's all about giving in a way that doesn't cause stress and receiving the love of others.

You can make your life easier and create your own heaven on earth right here, right now, by learning how to balance giving and receiving. You can give and receive in a whole new way—a way that honors and values Self and protects you from those who take more than they give.

The Power of Giving

Let's start our discussion with the power of giving, because few things in life are more satisfying than being able to give freely and from a full heart. This type of giving truly brings heaven to earth for everyone around you. And I'm not just talking about giving materially. Giving the gift of your time and your attention can be invaluable—to children, to animals, to other people. When my daughter had her first baby this past year, she was absolutely astounded by the graciousness of her friends who set up a meal train for her. She and her husband enjoyed a steady stream of homemade food left on their doorstep every day for several months. And those of us who made meals loved doing so. Giving of your time and attention to those in need—or just to give—feels fantastic when you do it healthfully.

I love hosting a good party to celebrate a milestone achievement or a birthday. And I have a particular knack for doing this in a way that brings people together. It's what Alexandra Stoddard, the author of *Living a Beautiful Life*, calls a "free space"—meaning some skill or gift you have that is effortless and comes naturally. When we give from our "free spaces" it costs us nothing. It energizes us. We are giving from a full cup.

Gifts of your time and attention that are obligations and duties, on the other hand, drain you. We are often made to feel guilty when we don't have the time or energy to volunteer or give our time and attention to a "worthy" cause. But our giving needs to include us. We need to give ourselves the resources to feel whole and replenished. Otherwise the well will eventually run dry. And we'll end up feeling resentment. And perhaps become bitter.

To give healthfully, you need to truly get in touch with yourself. Often we say yes to a request when we should say no because we don't want to face the consequences of saying no. We're worried that saying no will let someone down when we want to please them. Or perhaps we undervalue our time and energy and put the needs of others ahead of our own. Or we're worried that others will think we're selfish if we don't say yes. Or perhaps we just forget that our needs actually do matter—and they matter just as much as the needs of the other person.

But we all have to say no sometimes if we are going to keep ourselves healthy. To do this, we have to set benign boundaries in our giving and then stop when we reach those boundaries. You can do this graciously by saying, "Thank you so much for asking me, but I must say no to your request at this time." You also don't owe anyone a long explanation. Just say, "I simply can't." As Dr. Mario Martinez explains, "A benign boundary is reached when you can calibrate between resentment (you did too much) and guilt (you did not do enough). This embodied middle way allows you to take care of yourself without ignoring the needs of others. It's an action of what the Tibetan Buddhists call inclusive compassion: you are included in the compassionate act." What a brilliant solution!

Healthy Giving Process

When you've been asked to give something—whether a material gift, money, a service, or your time—go through this process to make sure that you are giving from a healthy place.

The first thing to do is notice your very first reaction when you were asked to give. If your gut gives a clear *heck yes!*, then, by all means, give! Similarly, if your gut gives you a clear *heck no!*, then steer clear. If the answer doesn't come immediately, however, you have to ask yourself some additional questions. In that case, simply say, "I'll get back to you. I have to think about it."

With uncertainty come questions. How does giving the gift make you feel? Does it fill you up in some way? Does it feel like an obligation? Why are you tempted to say yes? Why are you tempted to say no? When you think of giving the gift, do you feel tired and drained?

The important thing about all these questions is to see how the giving of the gift will really affect you. Are the negatives associated with giving it greater than the positives? And remember to think in the long term here. It's not simply about giving in this one instance. Constantly choosing the good of someone else over yourself will lead to poor health, which will be worse for everyone in the end. Honestly, unless you get that *heck yes!* in the beginning, the chances are pretty good that you should say no. Not always, but most of the time. Your gut knows what you need, and often the uncertainty you feel comes from your intellect butting in too quickly.

The Dark Side of Giving

While giving can be an amazing experience, there is also a dark side to it. Giving, in Western culture, is often where we place power. We get a lot of credit for giving, and so when we give on a regular basis, we can begin to look at ourselves as more important than those we give to. We can see this in families with a great deal of money.

The patriarch or matriarch holds all the power, and their children—and often their children's children—are at their mercy. The children give away their power in hopes of one day receiving an inheritance. There are too many stories of fully capable adults who have remained in limbo throughout their lives, never developing their gifts and talents because they are simply waiting for wealth. But even after their death, the person who had the means to give holds power. Through a will, they still decide who gets what and how much.

When I was doing some financial planning a few years back, I read the book *Beyond the Grave* by Gerald and Jeffrey Condon. The stories of what happens in families around inheritance were both eye-opening and downright tragic. Solid, well-educated families split apart when one sibling got more than the other, whether that meant the care of the family dog or Mother's engagement ring. I knew a woman who was utterly devastated by the fact that her sister got more of her deceased mother's jewelry than she did— despite the fact that they both inherited a fortune!

So remember, the giver tends to be in the power position. If you are on the receiving end, it's important to keep your power intact. Don't give yourself away in order to receive. And if you are always the giver, it's important to remember that giving should not be a way to control people. It should be done with an open heart in order to spread joy and prosperity to all parties.

You Were Born to Receive

As you can see, giving can lift you up energetically as long as you do it healthfully. Receiving is the same. Sadly, many of us don't know how to receive, even though we were fully dependent on it from the time we were growing in our mother's womb, receiving nourishing blood from the placenta through the umbilical cord. When we were born, that cord kept sending us oxygen as we made the massive changes necessary in our lungs and heart to breathe on our own. After that, we received nourishment and comfort from our mother's body, which acted as an external placenta. We could live only if we received. For many of us, this ability has been lost. Knowing how to receive fully and joyfully must be consciously remembered in adulthood.

But receiving graciously works in every area of your life, energetically speaking. Let's look at a physical example of this: Tighten your left fist as hard as you can. Tighten it until you can see the whitening of your knuckles from lack of circulation. Hold for the count of 10. As hard as you can. Now open your hand—palm up—and feel the circulation returning. Feels good, right? Your hand is now in the receiving mode. It's receiving oxygen, glucose, immune cells, electrolytes, and everything else that is carried in the blood. That is the power of receiving.

While this was a physical example, the same good feeling comes when you receive in any manner.

Do you remember being a kid and being so excited for Christmas morning or your birthday that you could barely sleep? That's the joy of receiving. These experiences were so pure. You hadn't yet been talked out of feeling this joy so passionately. Chances are you were so young that your joy wasn't tamped down by past experiences of feeling the crushing disappointment of not getting what you really wanted. And you hadn't learned that receiving has to somehow be earned. Our ability to receive openheartedly can be ruined by many different things.

Over the years many of us have been taught to "not get our hopes up" lest we be disappointed. This misguided guidance is intended to protect us from pain, but it really stems from the unresolved pain of those who have taught us this. And the pattern can be generations deep. The end result is living in a bandwidth of "not too happy and not too sad." A kind of middle ground free of downright sadness and disappointment but also free of amazing exuberance. We learn not to expect too much, and that becomes our daily reality. Over time, we end up believing that we don't deserve to receive—and therefore, we don't receive. As Amanda Owen writes in her book *The Power of Receiving*, "The only possible match for someone who doesn't know how to receive is someone who doesn't know how to give. Non-Receivers are drawn to non-Givers. In other words, the problem is not that you have been drawn to non-giving people, but that you are an inexperienced Receiver."

Worse yet, many of us were taught that we don't deserve to receive without giving something in return. As in "There's no such thing as a free lunch." This gives us the message that we are unworthy just as we are, which is completely untrue. Over my years of medical practice, I've seen countless instances in which the only way a woman can receive support, attention, and care from her husband and children is when she is sick. So guess what happens? She has to keep manifesting illnesses (albeit unconsciously) in order to keep receiving the attention and care that she should have been receiving anyway—in health, not just in sickness. I've also had numerous patients come to the realization that as children they had to get sick in order to receive their mother's attention. No wonder receiving can be so challenging! We've been taught that we have to earn it somehow. Through performing tasks that make us more worthy. Or through health problems or accidents. That's right. Studies show that even accidents are very often preceded by anger or sadness—emotions that let us know that we have a need that isn't being met. And so, given that often deep and unconscious programming about receiving, how can we begin to receive?

Receiving 101

Thank goodness receiving is actually a learnable skill—and a very worthwhile one. Being able to receive leads to a much more fulfilling life with more delight and joy than you might imagine possible.

Getting started is super simple. All you have to do is accept all compliments. When someone says, "Oh, I love your dress," your response should be "Thank you." That's it. Just thank you! Do not say, "I got it for five dollars at Goodwill." That downgrades the compliment and devalues the gift you just received. Also, resist the urge to return the compliment by saying something like, "Oh!

I like yours too." You do not have to give something back when you are complimented. By saying simply thank you, you have graciously received a compliment. You are slowly but surely getting on the path to being comfortable receiving.

An interesting thing will happen when you start to simply accept compliments. At first, you are apt to feel uncomfortable and vulnerable. You are out of practice. So when you notice that you're feeling uncomfortable, say to yourself, "I love you." That uncomfortable part needs more love, not less.

Once you're more comfortable receiving compliments—or even while you're still working with compliments—you can move on to some more advanced receiving practices. For example, in her book *Change Me Prayers*, Tosha Silver notes that you can say a Change Me Prayer to help rewire your brain to be better at receiving. You can say: "Divine Beloved, please change me into one who is willing to receive. Please change me into someone who knows her own worth. Please change me into someone who gratefully receives all that you have to offer me. Please change me into someone who provides others with the delight of giving to me."

In the box below, you'll see one of my favorite receiving practices. And I'm sure you can come up with many of your own. Just remember, the more you practice receiving, the better you'll get at it. And remember, the reason you have trouble receiving is because your inner child still believes he or she is not worthy of receiving. So just start by spending some time loving that part of you. Because that's all he or she wants anyway.

Compliments from the Natural World

I did this exercise years ago while gazing out my hotel room at Mount Rainier near Seattle, Washington. I was trying to prepare myself to go downstairs into a group of strangers at a medical meeting. But you don't have to have a mountain nearby to do it. Just think about a place in nature that you remember and love. All mountains, trees, and natural areas have big angelic presences associated with them.

Imagine that tree or mountain or flower speaking to you. It's telling you how wonderful you are. Simply listen as it says:

You are beautiful.

You are intelligent.

You are delightful and charming.

You are worthy.

And you are irresistible.

You are healthy.

Now breathe in these statements. Receive them right into your heart. Into your essence. And when you feel full, go about your day. But notice what happens.

For me, I noticed that when I walked out of my hotel room into the medical meeting, I was treated differently. Better. I received far more positive attention than I had before.

While I don't know that the circumstance I was in had changed a great deal, I do believe that because I flexed my receiving muscles (in the privacy of my own room) I was able to truly receive what had been there for me all along. I was astounded by this.

I'll never forget the first time I got a standing ovation for a lecture I gave. I felt as though I would fall off the back of the stage. I nearly cried. I didn't know what to do with all that energy coming my way. So I came home and took a long bath. My ability to receive was minimal back then. And my medical training—which encouraged getting by on no rest and no good food didn't help matters. Since then, I have consciously made it a point to stand and receive fully. To really take it in. To open my heart. Because here's what I know for sure: When my words touch an audience member or a friend, it is because those words are true for them too. Many times when I'm speaking publicly, I am actually articulating what others have always believed and felt too, but didn't quite have the ability to say. So my ability to receive their praise serves both of us. By receiving, I uplift and honor the giver fully. The circle is complete now. And all our vibrations rise together and the world gets brighter.

Receiving from Nature

When I think of the relationship between giving and receiving joyfully and openly, I look to nature. Mother Nature gives endlessly and bountifully, and we can all get in on receiving her gifts. This morning when I arose, the day was unseasonably warm, so I went outside in my bathrobe with bare feet. I allowed my feet to receive the negative ions from the earth herself, knowing that 20 minutes of standing on the earth decreases cellular inflammation in the body. Mother Earth gives this gift freely. I took it. With gratitude. And I gazed out across the river and simply received nature's glory—knowing that the warm days of autumn would soon be replaced by ice and snow.

On my way back to my house, I stopped and thanked a pink begonia outside my door. This plant had been providing me with beauty all summer. And for some reason, it hadn't stopped blooming for weeks, even though we were way past the usual killing frosts. Its location by the door had protected it. So I thanked it for providing me with so much color and joy for so many months. I received the love it was giving me.

Before I started writing, I went for a walk in the woods—and I made sure to remove my contact lenses before I went out. This way the autumn light would go directly into my brain via my retina. As I walked, I stopped and allowed myself to fully receive the sunlight. I even said a prayer of thanks to the Angel of the Sun. "Thank you dear Angel of the Sun for bathing me in your light. Please help me receive your glorious life-giving light into every cell of my body." With soft focus, I gazed at the golden leaves on the trees and allowed the rods and cones in my eyes to receive the vibrations from their colors. I received the soft breezes on my skin. I received the hilarious antics of two chipmunks wrestling and playing along the path. My walk was all about receiving everything that Mother Nature had to give me that day. I noticed that the apple trees had given their considerable bounty to the earth to replenish her soil—and also to feed the deer and squirrels. Mother Nature received this bounty and was soaking it in beautifully.

Mother Nature is constantly giving to us. We can learn by her example as we consciously attune to and receive these gifts. A sunset, a moonrise, a flower, a flock of birds, a grand view—all we have to do is be open to receiving.

Consciously Receiving from Nature

The late Peter Calhoun, the former Episcopal priest and shaman I mentioned in an earlier chapter, taught people how to walk in nature so that they might receive the gifts that are there for them. I was fortunate enough to have taken a workshop with him less than a year before he died. And this is what he taught us: Keep your eyes soft. Move very slowly. When you come to a tree that speaks to you, stop. And stand there. He said that tree spirits come out very slowly. And they are not used to having human attention. But human attention speeds up their evolution. Just stand there and love the tree. And allow it to love you back. Receive what the tree has to offer. Fully. Wholeheartedly. You might also gift the tree with some crystals or coins. Peter said that the nature spirits love this. You can do the same with stones, rocks, and other plants. And also bodies of water. When you raise your vibration in nature, all of Creation sings with you.

Matthew Fox, a priest, wrote a book called *Original Blessing* (in contrast to the doctrine of original sin). In it, he talked about how children—no matter how abused or lonely—often have a place in nature where they go to receive healing. A large rock, a special tree, a ravine. They can still feel the healing power that the earth is offering them. And they know how to receive it, no matter what else is going on.

And so, as you are opening yourself up to your own value and your ability to receive, start with Mother Nature. She'll never fail you.

The Gift of Gratitude

I spoke earlier about how receiving needn't be earned, and this is true. When you get that compliment, you do not have to give a compliment back. However, receiving fully and joyfully does bring with it another gift: the gift of gratitude. When you speak your appreciation to the giver of a gift, you raise both of your vibrations. You also help encourage the cycle of giving and receiving healthfully. By saying thank you, and really feeling it deep down in your Soul, you bring light and ease to a sometimes difficult topic.

One of the fastest ways to lose the goodness in your life is by lacking appreciation for it. On the other hand, being grateful for what you already have is a surefire way to get more. Gratitude is a way of being. It quite naturally raises your vibration and ability to attract because, by focusing on the abundance you currently have, you become a magnet for more of the same. Start by being grateful for things you might take for granted: a healthy body, food in the fridge, and a phone that works whenever you make a call. When you get into the gratitude habit, you begin to look around and see gifts and goodness all around you.

On New Year's Day of this year I was inspired by a post I found on Dr. Joe Dispenza's Facebook feed. It was written by a woman who'd started a gratitude journal, taking a picture of something she was grateful for each day over the course of an entire year. By the end of the year, she had transformed her relationship with her husband and her life—realizing how much her "glass half empty" attitude had colored her life beforehand. Her hashtag was #365grateful. Many people followed her example. I was so inspired by this that I decided it would be fun to make a little video on Instagram every day of the things I am grateful for. Because 2016 is a leap year, my Instagram hashtag has been #366gratitude. I have loved this practice. And I've discovered how easy it is to find things to take little videos of while speaking about why I'm so grateful for them. A walk in the woods, a sunset, my cat, my organized closet, my grandbaby and her family, firewood—the list goes on and on. And there's nothing like documenting it and sharing it with others to raise our collective vibration. This is also how I found the fairies visiting me as dancing light orbs on those videos I told you about in Chapter 4. Many people are doing this on social media. Gratitude is contagious. And it truly helps erase chronic negativity. Give it a try. A gratitude journal, a daily photo, or a bit of writing. You too will find yourself starting to see how heavenly life on earth can be.

CHAPTER 7

Keeping the Faith

*Faith is to believe what you do not see; the
reward of this faith is to see what you believe.*

— St. Augustine

Of all the qualities that truly make life easy, faith is the most important—and, I'll admit it, the most challenging. As I already mentioned, our current lives are created by a morphic field of energy and information left over from the past that attracts the circumstances of our present experience. We pick up learning our Soul's lessons in this lifetime where we left off in the last. And faith is what gives us the power to move forward on our journey. It is something we learn and earn over a lifetime.

Many years ago, when I was just getting started in my medical practice, I took what looked to me like a big leap of faith—working to create the new model of health care that I spoke about before. I wanted to empower people in their own health care, but to do so, I had to leave everything I knew and embark on a whole new way of working.

The decision to do this took root when I went to the empowerment workshop led by David Gershon and Gail Straub, the authors of *Empowerment.* David and Gail have spent their lives empowering people all over the planet—and in every circumstance—helping them tap into the power within them to create the life of their dreams. Their work was my first exposure to the universal laws of the universe—especially the law of attraction, which has since gotten a lot more exposure through books like *The Secret*.

Gail and David had us do affirmations on each aspect of our lives, including physical health, career, relationships, family, and so on. The laws of manifestation and attraction made absolute sense to me. They struck a chord of truth inside, much like when I had discovered the work of Edgar Cayce and the reality of angels. I completely believed that we create our own reality through the thoughts that we think and the feelings that result.

So there I was, a shiny new doctor, now armed with the tools for creating my own reality. Simple, right? Just get the affirmation right and the life you want will manifest. Easy peasy. Not so fast. I said my affirmations. I acted as if everything were going as it should. And yet our new medical center wasn't progressing as I imagined it. Not even close.

That's when I learned the power of faith. I had taken my leap of faith with specific outcomes in mind. But I soon realized that true faith was about letting go. I had to trust in the part of me that was orchestrating my circumstances from a higher perspective. This part of myself is not the same as the little self who is down here on earth managing day-to-day business, having to deal with crying children, being up all night with sick patients, and trying to get enough sleep. Still, being grounded in the truth of the law of attraction and how things manifest—albeit naively—gave me the courage to leave my conventional medical practice and co-create a new way of practicing medicine.

Ask the Divine for Help

There are basically two ways to live. One is in faith. The other is in fear. We are all taught to be afraid of just about everything. Afraid of growing older, gaining weight, being alone, contracting a virus, not wearing the right thing, running out of money, getting sick, and finally—the real monster in the closet—dying!

As previously mentioned, I have long been fascinated by those who've had near-death experiences. The latest account that has deeply touched me, which was written about in the book *Health Revelations from Heaven and Earth,* is that of Tommy Rosa, a former plumber from the Bronx who "died" in a hit-and-run accident when he was 40. Tony had an amazing time in heaven with a profound teacher who later revealed himself to be Jesus.

While in heaven, Tommy was taken to a beautiful sea with incredible blue water. He said that everything was vibrating and his Soul felt at home. But while he was treading water in the ocean with his Teacher, Tommy suddenly saw several large dark shapes barreling toward him. They were great white sharks, with big teeth and gaping wide-open mouths. His Teacher had disappeared, and Tommy went into utter panic as the sharks began to circle him. He knew he would be ripped to shreds by these monsters. And just when he thought his death was inevitable, he heard a strong, clear, calm voice in his head that said, "Have no fear."

Tommy sent back a mental message that amounted to: "Easy for you to say. You left me here to die."

Again the voice came back, this time stronger: "Have no fear."

So Tommy closed his eyes and worked on returning to inner peace and calm.

After several moments, he opened his eyes again, and to his great relief, the sharks had disappeared. Just like that.

He let out a huge sigh of relief, just as his Teacher materialized beside him and proceeded to teach him about the impact of the negative energy created by fear.

The long and short of this lesson is that whatever you're afraid of in life, you will attract to you. If you're afraid of illness, you will attract it. If you're afraid of being alone, you will be alone for as long as it takes to get over that fear. If you're afraid to die, you will never live fully and joyfully.

On a purely physical level, fear lowers our vibration and makes us far more susceptible to viruses and bacteria. The biochemical state that fear creates in our bodies adversely affects our immunity and increases our susceptibility to the pathological viruses and bacteria that are all around us. For example, the majority of us have the bacterium that causes pneumonia in our respiratory system at all times. But it stays in check until our vibration is lowered in some way. It's the same with nearly every other bacteria or virus we've been taught to be afraid of.

On an emotional level, fear blocks us from moving forward to the life of our dreams. An example is a woman who has been hurt in a relationship so doesn't dare to take a chance again; she just stays home by herself, lamenting her circumstances, too afraid to risk an attempt to change.

At its root, all fear results from a lack of faith—pure and simple. When you give in to your fear, you are not trusting the Divine. The only way to build the muscle of faith is to calm yourself and turn your trust over to God. Hence the saying "Let go and let God."

Turning fear into faith requires patience and commitment. Just telling someone to stop being afraid and to move into unshakable faith in their ability to live the life of their dreams is not helpful—especially if their nervous system has been imprinted with childhood trauma.

We often inherit our fears from our parents and their parents before them—imbibing them with our mother's milk—even if we can't pinpoint the reason for our own fears. It is well documented that babies can take on the fear of their mothers even in the womb.

Anxiety, like its close cousin depression, runs in families. And so do all the fears that keep it going. I have a good friend who was going through a lot of anxiety and fear having to do with his career recently, and he discovered that both of his parents, unbeknownst to him, were on medication for anxiety. I told him that that anxiety was not genetic; it was simply a pattern he had learned while growing up. But more important, I told him that he had the power to stop it. And stop it he has—through consistent effort to replace his fear with faith.

If you sincerely want your life to be easy, you simply must do what it takes to fire together new brain patterns based on faith.

How Faith Remodels the Brain

The same brain remodeling that happens as a result of choosing the thought that makes you feel better can happen when you start to live from a place of faith rather than fear. It's that whole "neurons that fire together, wire together" thing again. Faith-based thoughts of safety and security actually mold your brain and body to be more calm and peaceful. And the more you think and repeat these kinds of thoughts, the more the old wiring of fear and terror melts away. There is only so much of a chemical called neural growth factor that allows brain cells to wire in neuronal connections. So when you start creating neuronal connections associated with positive thoughts (*I feel safe and secure and connect with the healing power of Divine Love*), then the negative thought patterns (*I'm terrified I'll get cancer like my mother*) start to wither and die. And more than that, you begin to attract circumstances that reflect your new beliefs. The evidence of well-being begins to build.

In a culture and medical profession that is driven by the fear of everything that can go wrong—and in which so many community events are centered around "Running for a Cure"—it is no small task to keep firing your brain connections in positive ways. But the end result of becoming fear-resilient is worth every bit of effort you make to do so. Living in faith is infinitely more pleasant and productive than the opposite.

Fear: Your Ego's Way of Protecting You

To get a grip on your fear, you first need to understand the role of your ego. Remember from Chapter 1 that your ego is the part of you that got created by the stresses encountered in childhood and the subconscious beliefs developed from them. Your ego is not your real Self—the part that is directly connected with the Divine. The ego was created to protect you and also to give you the skills and judgment necessary to do what you came here to do. Your ego does what it does to protect you from feeling pain, loss, fear, and sorrow. And its primary MO is fear. You're not ever going to be able to fight your ego or the fearful scenarios it's always going to present to you. So the first step in living a life of faith is to not fight your fear. Or feel bad for having it.

In her wonderful book *Big Magic*, Elizabeth Gilbert talks about the fact that fear is going to be with you no matter what you do—especially if you want to live the life your Soul would like you to have, instead of the one your parents or society chose for you. So get used to the fact that fear is going along for the ride. Gilbert suggests thinking about fear as a family member on a road trip. It has to sit in the backseat. (You can decide whether or not to make it fasten its seat belt.) And it doesn't get to say anything. Or pick the route. Or change the radio station. Don't let it drink too much water either—otherwise it will constantly have to stop to use the bathroom. Just kidding.

Lack of faith tends to boil down to a belief that we are not worthy. Not worthy of love, acceptance, care, or understanding. Tommy, the plumber mentioned earlier, had a most amazing and detailed time in heaven with his Teacher. What he learned was precious, sacred, and profound. Life changing, in fact. And yet, eight years after he returned to life, he gained more than 100 pounds and developed heart failure. All of it stemming from a lack of self-love. He said that his ego just couldn't accept the fact that he was completely worthy of the kind of love and compassion that were shown to him in heaven. He was also too afraid of being ridiculed to share what he had learned, which he realized later was because of his ego. When I interviewed him on my radio show, he said that when he first shared his experience with his parish priest, the priest told his mother that he needed psychiatric help. Our fears are based on the truth of our experience—but we still have to transform them.

Most of us think that the ego is all about self-aggrandizement and bragging. But whether we are overinflating our importance or feeling unworthy, it's all still an ego trip fueled by fear. And the only way out is to have more faith in God and the Divine than we do in our own ego. Let me remind you that this dilemma is a big part of what this Earth school is here to teach us. And we pass the test only when our faith trumps our fear.

Stopping Fear before It Gains Momentum

There are quite a few practices that can help you reprogram your fear wiring, and we'll go into these soon, but we all need to learn how to arrest fear in the moment—before it takes over. Or reverse it when it has already begun. The last thing you need is for fear to grab the steering wheel from your hands. Much like a car that is on top of a hill and starts to roll a bit, you have to stop it before it picks up speed and accelerates down the hill.

Here's what I like to do when I notice that I'm feeling fear. I start by simply noticing it. I also scan my body and figure out where I feel the fear. Generally it's in my solar plexus. Then I say to my fear: "I love you. You are precious. I know you're afraid. I will take care of you." This instantly breaks the fear trance.

Then I take a long, deep, slow breath through my nose and hold it for a couple of seconds. Then I exhale slowly through my nose, allowing the exhale to be longer than the inhale. I repeat this three times, and then I have fully stopped the fight-or-flight fear response in my body. I have turned on the rest-and-restore parasympathetic nervous system.

This is such a simple practice.

Becoming Fear Resilient

Moving from a life of fear to a life of faith takes a lot of focus. Yes, you can now stop fear in its tracks when it takes you by surprise, but this in itself will not remodel your brain. It's a great start, don't get me wrong, but it takes more than that to change your thinking.

The teacher Abraham, as channeled by Esther Hicks, answers a lot of questions from individuals who reach out only once they are in crisis. Abraham likens that to someone who jumps out of a plane, finds that the parachute isn't working, and then says, "What should I do?" The standard answer is "Don't worry. It will be over soon." It's so much easier to prevent a crisis than to deal with it once it's already under way. The key is to notice and attend to your fears when they are just creeping in.

There are many ways of stopping fear from creeping in. Three of the most useful I've found are practicing courage, prayer, and tapping.

Practicing Courage

When you're learning to move forward in faith, don't sabotage yourself by trying to tackle the biggest fear of your life. For example: "I'm 39 and haven't yet met the man of my dreams. I really want to have a baby. But I'm afraid I'm running out of time." Start small. Let's say you're afraid of rejection or afraid to ask for help. You can mentally practice a scenario that takes you to the brink of this particular fear so you can work through the emotions associated with it.

Let's take the fear of rejection as an example. Imagine yourself walking into a coffee shop. You see an attractive man or woman standing at the counter about to order. Someone who looks approachable. Now imagine going up to them and saying hello. Here's all you have to do. Say, "Hi." That's it. Imagine doing that, and go over it several times in your head. Imagine different people in front of you.

What did you notice about that exercise? Did your palms get sweaty? Did your breath speed up? Did your throat get dry? What did you notice? Did you get rejected? Or were you pleasantly surprised?

Repeat this exercise daily for seven days. It only takes about 15 seconds, so trust me, you've got the time to do it. After one week of "practice" in your head, go do it. Go to a coffee shop. Or store or wherever you usually go. And actually say hi to a stranger. See what happens.

You can do the same thing if you're afraid to ask for help. Bring to mind someone you could call to ask for help. Who is the first person that comes to mind? Is there another one as well? Write down their names.

Now make a list of things you'd like help with if the world were perfect and you weren't afraid of rejection. It could be anything: cleaning out the basement, grocery shopping, doing laundry, holiday shopping, going to a concert, keeping you company on a road trip, listening to a poem you wrote, going to lunch together, and so on.

Now pick one. Next, pick up the phone and pretend you are calling to ask for help. Make it as real as you can. Make up a script so you know what to say. For example: "Hi, Joe. There's something I'd like you to help me with, but I'm terrified to ask." And then dive into the request. "Is there any way you'd be willing to help me take a load to the recycling center? I know you go there regularly. Would it be possible for you to swing by my house and pick some stuff up for me?"

Now that you've practiced, try it for real. You will be amazed how often people say yes when you ask for help. Not all the time, but often enough.

Having little triumphs that prove to you that you can have faith in someone or in God begins to build your faith muscle.

The Power of Prayer

Dr. Larry Dossey, an internist and the author of *Healing Words: The Power of Prayer and the Practice of Medicine,* has documented how effective prayer is for helping us improve the conditions of our daily lives—including healing help. Prayer has been shown, among many other things, to increase conception rates in couples with infertility, and also to decrease the number of days in the intensive care unit for heart attack patients. It even helps plants grow better. In general, there is nothing that isn't helped by prayer.

There are more than 300 peer-reviewed studies on the healing power of prayer, and it turns out that prayer is effective no matter what your belief system or religion. It also doesn't matter what kind of prayers you use. What matters is your sincere desire to connect with the Divine.

I remember reading one of Anne Lamott's books a while back. As I recall, she said that the two best prayers she knows are "Help me, help me, help me" and "Thank you, thank you, thank you."

In his wonderful book *Angel Prayers*, Kyle Gray says that he always begins his prayers with "Thank you, [angel], for your help in [this matter]." So let's say you want help from Archangel Raphael, who is known for his healing power. The prayer would be "Thank you, Archangel Raphael, for sending me your healing energy and for assisting me in shoring up my faith in my ability to be well."

Tosha Silver's Change Me Prayers can also go a very long way in bypassing the death grip of fear and enlisting Divine help in building faith. This is especially true with the big fears that keep you up at night. The ones that you simply can't seem to get around—no matter what you do.

Change Me Prayers for calming fear and strengthening faith can be very simple. For example: "Change me, Divine Beloved, into someone who trusts that my needs will always be met." Or "Change Me, Divine Beloved, into one who truly trusts. Change me into one whose fear melts away like dew in the sunlight. Strengthen my faith in you and in the fact that all things will work out for me. Always."

Tap Away the Fear

Another very effective way to deal with fear is through tapping—also known as Emotional Freedom Techniques, or EFT. Since fear sets up an electromagnetic field that attracts the things you fear, you need a way to change that electromagnetic field. That's what tapping does. It actually assists in removing the neuromuscular tension in the body that is being held in place by our fear—both conscious and unconscious. As a result, tapping helps us release fear from our bodies, and in the process it lowers stress hormones.

To do EFT, you start by naming your problem but also add a positive affirmation while using your fingertips to tap on acupressure points that are based on the 12 major energy meridians of the body. These are the same points that have been used in traditional acupuncture for more than 5,000 years.

When the healthy flow of energy becomes blocked in your meridians, it also becomes blocked in your physical body. By tapping on the energy points linked to a specific organ or system, you put energy directly into that meridian. You also calm the amygdala, the primitive part of the brain involved in the fight-or-flight response. The use of the positive statement—such as "I have everything I need within me to feel safe, secure, and loved"—works to clear your meridians and any emotional blocks from your body's bioenergy system, bringing it back into balance.

Tapping helps you deal with way more than fear (though fear is often at the base of all our woes). No matter what your dilemma—whether illness, grief, pain, fear, financial distress, or excess weight, or if you just want to be more effective in stating and implementing your goals—tapping can help. It's all about recognizing the problem and then working through the events or emotions associated with it.

Here's how to perform EFT on yourself:

1. **Remove Eyeglasses and Jewelry.** When possible, remove eyeglasses and jewelry that you cannot easily tap around. Jewelry, especially some gemstones, can also interfere electromagnetically with your efforts.

2. **Figure Out What's Ailing You.** Before you can begin tapping, you must figure out what you are trying to remedy in your life. For example, you may feel nervous about flying. Or you might be afraid to ask someone for help. It could even be that you have physical pain that seems to be hindering your life.

3. **Assess Your Level of Physical or Emotional Discomfort.** Once you've pinpointed what's wrong, rate your current level of discomfort about that

situation on a 1-to-10 scale, with 1 meaning that it barely affects you and 10 meaning that it's creating a lot of problems. Be sure to assess your *current* level, not a past level. Don't worry too much about your number. Just note whatever comes to mind. You will do this assessment before and after you tap and use the numbers as a way to see progress.

4. **State Your Affirmation.** Always begin your tapping session by stating a positive affirmation to clear any subconscious negative thoughts. Use the following phrase: "Even though I [state your condition or situation], I deeply and completely love and accept myself." So if you are afraid that you won't be able to pay off your college debt, you'd say, "Even though I'm afraid I can't pay off my debt, I deeply and completely love and accept myself." If you're not comfortable saying that you love yourself, you can end your affirmation with the phrase, "I am okay" instead. Be as specific as you can. Try naming the root cause of the emotion or the event that is causing you pain.

5. **Create a Reminder Word or Phrase.** As you're tapping through the points, you will not use the full affirmation. Instead you will create a reminder word or phrase to state. This shortened version of the issue you are addressing will keep it front and center in your mind. So for the college debt situation, your phrase could be something like, "this loan" or "this fear."

6. **Use Your Fingertips.** Your fingertips have a number of energy meridians. Typically, you use your index and middle finger to tap.

    Start at the karate chop point, which is on the outside of your hand, where you'd break a board with a karate chop. Tap here while repeating the affirmation several times.

Then move on, using one or both hands, and tap firmly between five and nine times on each point, in the following sequence, while repeating your reminder word or phrase. Tap the basic sequence below for two rounds.

- Eyebrow: the place right at the top of your nose where your eyebrow begins

- Side of the eye: immediately to the outside corner of your eye, not yet to the temple

- Under the eye: at the top of the bone directly under your eye

- Under the nose: in the divot under the nose

- Chin: in the indent between your mouth and your chin

- Collarbone: under the collarbone, in the center of one side

- Under the arm: in the midline, where a bra strap would be

- Top of the head: in the center (think of looking like a monkey)

7. **Reassess Your Level of Discomfort.** After tapping for two rounds, check in with the number you gave yourself at the beginning for the level of discomfort you felt. Notice whether the anxiety or pain or whatever has decreased. It usually does very quickly. If your number has gone down dramatically, your tapping has done its job. However, if you have only partial relief, do some more rounds of tapping. If some new source of discomfort has surfaced since you began, tap on that. For example, you may have felt fear before, but after tapping you feel great sadness. In this instance, you would now tap on the sadness. If your discomfort stems from the same issue that

you originally tapped on, simply use the phrase, "Even though I still [state your issue], I deeply and completely love myself."

8. **Listen and Notice.** When you complete your tapping session, take a deep breath, sit quietly, and listen. You'll likely notice that some kind of guidance has come in that you couldn't hear when you were in the swamp of fear. An example might be something like this: "Even though I was very afraid I couldn't pay off my loan, I have now remembered some resources available to me. I am feeling some relief. And am happier about all of it." Often answers or resolutions begin to arise spontaneously from deep within you. This happens within a couple of minutes. Notice how you no longer feel stuck and powerless because tapping gets you out of your intellect and into your own heart and your own wisdom.

If you are working with tapping on your own, you can find all sorts of resources to learn more about it. Simply Google "tapping" or "EFT"—you'll find more information than you probably want, including free video tutorials and all kinds of scripts you can tap along with. I know a lot of people watch videos of tapping on You-Tube before they begin, just to get a feel for the process.

If you are interested in working one-on-one with an EFT professional, you can find certified practitioners at www.eftuniverse .com/certified-eft-practitioners. If you do work with someone, they will likely help you craft a script that is very specific to your issues.

The important thing to remember is that healing through tapping isn't based on strict rules. You don't have to worry about getting the affirmation *just right.* Just make sure you aren't denying what you need to work through. And while no technique or procedure works for everyone every time, studies show that people who use tapping for a specific problem experience significant improvement. And their cortisol levels also plummet. That in itself makes tapping worthwhile, since cortisol is linked with cellular inflammation, and cellular inflammation is the root cause of almost all chronic degenerative diseases like arthritis, diabetes, heart disease, and cancer.

If you decide to use tapping to clear up your fears around money, health, relationships, or any other area of your life, remember that your beliefs about your worthiness or lovability are almost always the core issue. I have been there in every area from money to relationships. I have changed my beliefs. You can do the same. None of this happened overnight. But as my fears have arisen over the years, I have been able to gradually make them give way to confidence and self-love. This has opened an entirely new world of friends, fun, and financial literacy. And I have more faith than ever before.

Surrender and Offering

It's relatively easy to live in faith when nothing really bad has ever happened to you. But sooner or later, all of us will experience something that seriously tests our faith. You find out that your spouse is having an affair, your house burns down and you lose everything, or you or a loved one is diagnosed with a terminal illness. And the list goes on.

These are the events that truly separate the faithful from the fearful.

Many times these painful events are actually orchestrated by the Soul to assist us in moving from fear to faith. It's enormously helpful to realize that, on some level, everything that happens to you is designed to help your spiritual evolution. Despite the difficulties and opposition I have encountered along my path in transforming the way women see their bodies and their health, it has all been worth it. But it has taken effort. And commitment. Whether or not your life is easy has a lot to do with how you handle loss, failure, accidents, shame, conflict, and illness.

Are you going to let a loss or accident cripple you emotionally for the rest of your life? Or are you going to use it to build unshakable faith? All painful emotions have a gift within them. Grief pulls heaviness out of us. It lightens us if we simply allow ourselves to grieve. Is it uncomfortable? You bet. Is it worth it? Yes. The choice to receive the gift of discomfort and inconvenience is yours. And your choice will either help you create heaven on earth, or just the opposite . . . it will send you into the low vibration of hopelessness and helplessness that we refer to as a living hell.

Faith that things happen for a reason is really the only way through. I've lost two sisters. The first when I was quite young—only about five. The second one when I was in my Saturn Return during my medical residence. When I got the news that she died in a car accident on her way home from teaching a gymnastics class, I was completely devastated. It felt as though lightning had struck my life. Life would never be the same. But I also knew that this was a time to practice what I had always preached. I had to surrender to a greater plan and remember that our Souls are immortal—we don't die. I knew I would see my sister again one day. That eased my grief and gave this loss meaning. But I still cried myself to sleep for months. It took my mother far longer to come to peace with this loss, though she once said, "I don't think I'll ever get over it completely. And that's okay."

When you are up against a fear or a loss that has you in its grip, I can assure you that you are going to have feelings about it—anger, sorrow, sadness, fear. And, like my mom said, that's okay. It's not only okay; it's the only way for the Soul to do what it came to do. What you don't want is to remain permanently stuck in bitterness, anger, or chronic grief. While you're here on earth, you have to live your life here—no matter what. That's the contract.

Tosha Silver's life work involves teaching people how to offer everything to the Divine. Everything. That means that you say to the Divine, "Okay. I am yours. And the relationship that's driving me nuts is also yours. I offer it all to you, including my body, my health, and my lover who just left me." The way to loosen our grip on anything is to realize that none of it really belongs to us. It all belongs to the Divine part of ourselves. Tosha tells the story of a woman who had to be evacuated from her house because there were wildfires in the area. She was incredibly attached to the house and everything in it. She didn't think she could bear to part with it. But over the next few days, while firefighters fought the fires and she stayed with a friend, she kept repeating, "My house is *yours*, Divine Beloved. It doesn't belong to me. I turn it all over to *you*. Help me to let it go." It took her several days of this as she burned through her attachment to the house. Later she found out that the fire had stopped just before her house. She had been willing to offer her house and the outcome to the Divine—and then didn't have to.

How often have you had this happen in your life? You finally come to grips with something that you have to release, and then you find that your willingness to release it magically released the problem. Of course, by then you have changed your vibration from fear to faith! You've surrendered your attachment. You've offered it all to the Divine. Jesus's last words on the cross were "Father—into thy hands, I commend my fate." We all have the ability to do this. It's a process, not an event. It's not intellectual. And it requires love and patience.

In yogic philosophy, there is the concept of samskaras, or attachments that must be burned away. There are many approaches that can help with this. Just know that the process of burning away long-held attachments—such as to a lover who left—can be incredibly painful. It quite literally feels like you are being burned. What is really happening, though, is that you are burning away attachments that keep you stuck.

When you practice true surrender and offer everything to the Divine—over and over and over—you will eventually discover true spaciousness and peace opening up before you and within you. You will have transformed your fear into faith.

do you think you are, Little Miss Perfect? No one goes to college in this family. Do you think you're better than we are?"

Your tribe keeps you safe as long as you believe what they believe and behave as they behave. In ancient times, tribes actually lived in enclosures known as pales, which protected their members as long as they stayed in the enclosed area. But once their members stepped "beyond the pale," then the tribe would no longer protect them. As Dr. Mario Martinez so beautifully documents in his book *The MindBody Code*, when we have the courage to step "beyond the pale" of our own tribe, the tribe usually wounds us through abandonment, betrayal, or shame—both to keep us safe and to keep us under control. Sadly, the rules of the tribe often don't match the dictates of our Souls, so living by these rules can also hurt our sense of self-worth. It can be a lose-lose situation if your tribe and your Soul are at odds.

I was working with an artist recently who discovered her knack for cutting hair when she was about 12. She was so good at it that her girlfriends often came over to get a new haircut. But her father, a strict Catholic, thought that spending time on personal beautification—or even making art—was a sinful waste of time. So she felt she had to hide all her artistic endeavors from him. If he happened to see her cutting someone's hair out on the lawn (she didn't dare do it in the house), he'd shame her for wasting time. And blame her for disobeying his wishes. His disapproval of her innate gifts and talents made her feel unworthy. Thank goodness she finally listened to her Soul's direction and left home. Eventually she became a successful artist and felt her intrinsic worth.

Many families have all kinds of implied rules and regulations that are unspoken. And a child learns about them only when they have crossed a line—a line that was never mentioned before. The well-studied alcoholic family system is a great example. This system runs on unspoken rules that a child is supposed to intuit without ever having them explained. The child feels underlying tension from the secrecy within the family. Mom gets drunk regularly and the child knows that something is wrong. But the adults won't talk about it, so the child blames herself and then either acts out her frustration destructively—by using drugs and alcohol herself later on—or becomes Little Miss Perfect.

When we are shamed as children, that shame becomes internalized. We end up believing that we are flawed and unworthy of the connection we so desperately seek. Because we so often feel ashamed and unworthy, we have an insatiable need for approval from others, a need to feel like we belong. And it's very easy to bond with others not from our strengths and our glory—but instead over the parts of ourselves that have made us feel like victims: our wounds, our illnesses, our weaknesses.

Because of this shame, we begin to live in a world filled with blame, anger, and guilt, and living from this place keeps us stranded in disconnection and worthlessness.

Narcissism and Personality Disorders

The cycle of shame, anger, and guilt is often fueled by our relationships—both our love relationships and our friendships. There is one type of relationship—above all others—that can create immeasurable amounts of shame and guilt: relationships with people who have personality disorders.

People who are narcissistic, borderline, and antisocial do enormous amounts of damage to the people with whom they have relationships. While each of these personality disorders is defined differently, they all have narcissism in common. Having a narcissistic parent, spouse, relative, boss, or sibling can leave even the most accomplished people feeling inadequate and crazy. Interestingly, it is the people who are the most skilled in their lives—and the most empathetic—who tend to attract these human vampires. The research of Sandra Brown, author of *Women Who Love Psychopaths: Inside the Relationships of Inevitable Harm with Psychopaths, Sociopaths & Narcissists*, has found that this is especially true for women with "super traits" of empathy and skill. These women, who are often lawyers, doctors, or CEOs of profitable companies, are attracted to narcissists because they feel like they can fix them. Why not? They're good at everything else. But they can't. Individuals with personality disorders do not change. Ever. Okay—maybe someone somewhere has, but the only time you see it consistently is in the movies. Real-life narcissists just move on to their next source of "narcissistic supply." While Brown's work focuses on women, I have met plenty of men in relationships with narcissistic women or those with borderline personality disorder. Try as they might, these men find it impossible to do right by their women, who use them for financial gain and then move on.

Narcissistic abuse is very common in our society; in fact, Sandra Brown calls it the number one unrecognized public health problem of our time. And, quite frankly, the mental health profession tends to gloss over it—probably because there are no reliable and effective treatments. But we need to look at it because it strengthens the blame/guilt knot in those people who experience it.

The kind of person who is most drawn to spirituality and self-help is quite often the kind of person who is targeted by a narcissist. Narcissists are charming, seductive chameleons who home in on the wounds of their victims and then tell them exactly what they know the victim is longing to hear. "Where have you been all my life? You are the most beautiful woman [handsome, strong man] I have ever met." They use their charm and skill to appear as the "perfect" partner. But after a while, the false persona created by their egos falls away—an ego usually can't keep up a front for more than a couple of years. Then their real characteristics begin to shine through, and then there is no pleasing them. Normal empathetic individuals make the mistake of thinking that the narcissist has the same empathy and remorse that they do. They believe that with enough love and caring the narcissist will come around. But they don't.

Those who are suffering from narcissistic abuse tend to blame themselves for all the problems in the relationship and continue to "work on themselves" in an effort to make the relationship work or make the narcissist change. They believe that if he (or she) just read this book, or went to this conference, or read this article, then surely he (or she) would "get it" and change. But all this does is drain the energy of the empathetic person while feeding the narcissist who is keeping them on the line by giving them just enough to keep them hooked. The empathetic person thinks, *Oh—now he "gets it." He's getting better.* But the only thing he "gets" is that he has to pretend to "get it" so that she stays.

Narcissists can ruin the people with whom they're in relationships, adding to their pain, shame, and guilt. They drain their victims dry, belittle them, and make them begin to doubt their own worth. You can often tell a couple in which one is a narcissist. The narcissist looks great physically, while the person with empathy (their supply) looks tired and overweight. If you are in a relationship like this, the sooner you recognize it, the better. To make life easy, you must learn how to spot a narcissist, and eventually stop focusing on why your partner has these traits. You must stop trying to help because you are simply "donating blood" instead of living your own life. They have their own Higher Power. You aren't it.

Now, having said that, please understand that a part of you—your Soul—brought these individuals into your life to help you find and stand in your worthiness and your personal power. Once you name and recover from narcissistic abuse, you'll find that your life is easier and more fun than you ever thought possible. But it's a process, not an event. And society has, for centuries, tended to protect narcissists, many of whom are very brilliant at what they do. So we make excuses for how they treat others.

When you first wake up to the reality of narcissistic abuse, it can be shocking, and you might not want to believe it. But you must—and then do whatever it takes to stop reacting to the narcissist and start living your own life. If you don't, you will continue to be shoved back into the blame/guilt knot that blocks an easy life. I've listed some good resources to help you in the resource section.

Searching for Meaning

When we have been living a life that inflicts shame on us, we often shut down and disconnect from our Divine selves. Our egos, which were created to protect us from the pain of this disconnection and from the pain of leaving our innate oneness consciousness, take over. They go on a search for meaning in our daily experiences of shame, and one way they do this is to identify with one of three predefined archetypal roles: victim, persecutor, or rescuer. Victims are those who take no responsibility, putting the blame for their life circumstances on everyone and everything else: "It's not my fault I'm overweight; it's genetic." Persecutors take full responsibility, but not in a loving way: "It's all my fault I'm overweight. I shouldn't eat so much cake. I'm a slob." And rescuers evade the situation by focusing on helping others with their problems: "Weight? Forget that, I need to focus on this plan to build a school in Africa."

While none of these roles addresses problems healthfully, they each provide an excuse to not fix what's wrong. They give you a place. A purpose. Meaning.

At various times, we have all been in each of these roles. That's part of being human. But to live heaven on earth you have to step out of them and take the bigger view. Most people can readily relate to the victim or rescuer role. But few of us are willing to step up and admit that sometimes we have been the persecutor. I certainly don't know any parent, myself included, who hasn't lashed out at their child and wounded them in some way. I vividly recall how once, at the end of my rope after a long day at work, I couldn't get my oldest daughter (then six months old) to stop crying. I was crying and shaking her car seat and yelling at her, "What do you want from me?" Yikes. I have since apologized.

Running for the victim or rescuer role while assiduously avoiding the persecutor role and denying that you've ever hurt anyone or yourself does nothing to help you. Every single one of us has had to play the heavy and "fire" someone in their life—not contact them, not invite them to the party, disappoint them in some way. And no matter what you do to explain your position, you're still going to be seen as "the bad guy." There's no way around it.

There is absolutely no power to change anything in your life as long as you chronically occupy one of these three positions.

Way back in the 1980s, the well-known medical intuitive Caroline Myss did a reading for me. She said, "You are a rescue addict, do you hear me? Your heart rhythm has changed over the past year. You've got to stop that behavior." I knew, deep in my heart, that she was correct. I had placed myself in the role of rescuer and, by doing so, often forgot that all people have a Higher Power—a Divine Self that provides them with direct access to their own unique inner guidance. I sometimes forgot, given my medical training, that I was not the Higher Power of my patients. Because, believe me, being a skilled rescuer who always has the answers for another is one pretty amazing ego trip. But this is just as unhealthy as always being a victim or a persecutor.

Physical Manifestations of Shame, Blame, and Guilt

Stepping out of the roles of victim, persecutor, or rescuer is not only good for you emotionally; it is necessary for good physical health. Feeling ashamed of something and not being able to talk about it and release it produces an inflammatory chemical in the body called interleukin-6 (IL6). Cellular inflammation from this and other pro-inflammatory chemicals in the body sets the stage for all chronic degenerative diseases including cancer, heart disease, and arthritis. And as you saw in my own situation, playing rescuer all the time was adversely affecting my health. My drive to save women from unnecessary hysterectomies, C-sections, and all kinds of other things was, quite literally, hurting my own heart.

Over my many years in clinical practice, I've had to find a way to support people in accessing their inner power to heal, which involves engaging every part of them—body, mind, and Spirit. Releasing shame is the first step in this. If they aren't able to do this, they aren't able to accept the fact that they have the power to create a healthier reality. The ego takes over and they simply fall back into their roles. They become victims exclaiming that they're not to blame for their illness or circumstances, which also means that they can't change it. Or they become persecutors, accepting full blame for their lives, and in turn wallowing in their perceived inability to change. Or they move to the rescuer role and distract themselves entirely from the situation.

When the ego has taken over the steering wheel of life, it's really going to bristle anytime anyone suggests that we have the power to create our own reality. Especially when it comes to our health, which we've been told we have no control over. And this makes perfect sense. Our egos are protecting us. The problem is that they are also preventing us from accessing our power to truly flourish.

The part of us that is creating the illness or imbalance is not the part that is having to deal with it at a lower vibration here on earth. It's a combination of unresolved childhood pain plus Soul lessons we came to learn.

To resolve any health problems you have or any negativity you feel, you must be willing to look deeply into the beliefs and behaviors that have resulted in your current life circumstances. You have to take the 10,000-foot view and rise above the situation.

Your power to change is always in the present moment. When you learn that there is a great deal you can do to change your thoughts, emotions, and behavior and thus change your circumstances—and even your health—you are empowered. All of us have enormous power to change our lives for the better if we're willing to step out of the powerless stance of our ego roles.

Rising Above

Taking the 10,000-foot view calls for you to find the larger truth in any situation and understand that every situation is an opportunity for spiritual growth. Remember that these circumstances were set up by the Divine part of you before you were born. For example, one of the most sobering—and liberating—situations in my medical career involved being reported to the Board of Registration in Medicine by a general surgeon who didn't like that I had disagreed with his opinion that his patient needed surgery for bowel cancer. He had seen a woman named Helen when she developed narrowing of her stool and some abdominal pain. He was unable to insert a sigmoidoscope very far up her colon, and so he was certain she had bowel cancer and required surgery as soon as possible. Helen came to see me for a second opinion because after she began a macrobiotic diet, all her symptoms had gone away. She felt better than she had in years. I told her that I knew of one well-documented case of stage 4 bowel cancer that had been cured by a macrobiotic diet, but I couldn't assure her that she didn't have cancer. So instead she agreed to keep eating the macrobiotic diet and then have all her tests repeated in a couple of months at another institution. I wrote to her surgeon, explaining the course of action we had agreed upon. Furious, he wrote a letter to my medical board saying, "Is it the standard of practice of medicine in Maine to treat bowel cancer with a macrobiotic diet?"

Needless to say I was completely terrified. Even though the patient herself had written to the board and assured them that she was in complete agreement with this approach, I wasn't so sure that the board would go along with her right to choose this option. I developed a pit in my stomach that went on for weeks. And I prayed, knowing that if I could heal this situation inside me it would likely go away outside of me. (Recall the "Surrender and Offering" section from Chapter 7.) Back then the board met about every three months to review complaints, so I knew it would take a while for my "sentence" to be issued.

I walked around for weeks fearing that my medical license would be taken away by the powers that be. After all, back then any doctor who even suggested that nutrition had anything to do with health was considered a quack. But I held firm to my conviction that I had to practice medicine that supported the right of a patient to have dominion over her own body. And besides, I had seen many medical miracles resulting from a change in diet and lifestyle—in people who had been turned away by the medical profession who had nothing else to offer them.

One day while I was doing proprioceptive writing (see Chapter 5) to gain clarity, peace, and understanding of this issue, I began to spontaneously write a letter to this surgeon. A wave of compassion and understanding came over me. And I forgave him. I told him that I understood that his motivation was Helen's well-being. He was only doing what he considered proper and right. And when I was finished with that write, that feeling of dread in my solar plexus was gone. Something had shifted within me. I was no longer a victim. When I went into the hospital the next day, I met a colleague at the coffee urn. He served on the Board of Registration in Medicine. And he said to me, "Oh, have you heard? The board unanimously decided to drop that case. The surgeon was way off. Your patient had every right to choose her own course of treatment." Needless to say, I was relieved. I was also relieved that the results of Helen's repeated tests were all normal. There was no evidence of any bowel cancer.

Owning Your Story

As I mentioned earlier, the first step of untying the blame/guilt knot is letting go of shame. If you can't do this, you'll always move back into those archetypal roles of victim, persecutor, or rescuer, which take away your power to control your own life.

Remember the story I told you in Chapter 7 about Tommy Rosa, the plumber who had the stunningly beautiful and reassuring near-death experience? Well you would think that after going to heaven, knowing that we don't die, and being taken around by one of the greatest teachers of all time—Jesus—that Tommy would have come back to earth and had a totally fabulous life from then on, right?

The truth was that Tommy still had a boatload of shame from his childhood programming. Who was he to have had such an incredible experience? Who was he to have been worthy of such a profound and loving Teacher showing him incredible information about health and healing? Tommy's unhealed shame is what his near-death experience didn't heal. He had to come back and transform that on his own.

I have another good friend named John who "died" from an overdose of narcotic pain medication, which had been prescribed for pain relief following a shoulder injury. John, who has a long history of drug and alcohol abuse, had been clean and sober for a year, but this drug set him back very quickly. And when he showed up at the hospital knowing that he needed help, his heart stopped. Twice. And he had to be resuscitated. I saw him shortly after this, and he was truly illuminated from within. A different person. Almost literally glowing with Spirit.

And he said, "Archangel Michael saved me." He didn't know much about Archangel Michael at the time, but he was sure that this had been the case.

But despite quite literally being pulled back from death's door by Archangel Michael, and despite being able to feel that powerful angel's presence for months afterward, John had a hard time accepting that he was worthy of being saved. *Why me? Why would this powerful being save me?* John's Irish Catholic background, plus the neglect of his parents when he was little, all contributed to him feeling ashamed and unworthy.

Shame thrives in darkness, in secrecy. It is a low, slow vibration that keeps us trapped by the belief that we're not enough. That we don't belong. That we are fatally flawed. Kind of like the main character in Alice Walker's *The Color Purple*, who has been raped and beaten for years. Through the love of another woman, she begins to feel her own worth and realizes that she does not deserve bad treatment—and she never did. Through this realization, the spell is broken, and she finds the courage to free herself from abuse. The only thing that changed was her. Nothing else. Just her. Same thing goes for Tina Turner when she finally walked out on her abusive husband, Ike, with only 10 cents to her name.

We have more power within us to change than we have been led to believe. And it all starts with owning our stories. As Brené Brown writes, "Owning our story can be hard but not nearly as difficult as spending our lives running from it." In order to untie the blame/guilt knot and live heaven on earth, you have to be willing to take responsibility for yourself and your circumstances. And if there is something you didn't know before but know now, you act on the new knowledge and fix what needs fixing if possible.

One of my favorite examples of this comes from my childhood. I grew up in a small town. One day my father got a call from the local pharmacist, who was contacting him to let him know that my sister had stolen some penny candy. Because she got caught, she had to endure the shame of returning the candy, but she also learned right from wrong. She learned that her behavior was wrong, but not her worth as a human being. She also learned that you sometimes have to take responsibility for your actions to make things right.

While my parents handled this situation in a positive way— keeping the focus on her behavior and not her intrinsic worth— many people don't. If you grew up in an unloving home where you were routinely shamed for your behavior, it's likely that this distinction wasn't made.

How to Release Shame

Think of something you are ashamed of. Something you have never told anyone. Something you think is so awful that you can't share it. Maybe you stole something as a kid and never told anyone. Or you found yourself feeling pleasure when you were being sexually molested. Or you have been addicted to porn. Or you were part of a mean-girls group in school and bullied other girls. Or maybe there's something about your body that you're ashamed of. Or your family. Maybe you're ashamed of your parents. Whatever it is, know that the longer you keep it hidden, the more damage it will do to you.

It's very easy to bring more love into the place where the shame currently lives. You simply state out loud the thing that you are so ashamed of. Do that now. Simply say, "I am so ashamed of myself for [blank]." Now look in the mirror and say out loud, "I love you right there." This actually brings the Infinite Love of your Divine Self right into the darkness and isolation of your shame. And illuminates it into Love.

To make this exercise even more effective, repeat it with a trusted friend. Tell him or her what you are ashamed of. And have them say to you, "I love you right there." The shame will

> melt away like dew in the sunlight. And what's more, you will have "grown up" the scared child inside of you who never dared speak her truth.

Owning your story not only helps you release shame but also increases feelings of self-worth. Stepping up and saying that you're wrong when you actually are is much more effective than being defensive and getting your ego all puffed up. A while back, for example, Dr. Bernie Siegel, author of *Love, Medicine & Miracles*, and I were co-presidents of the American Holistic Medical Association. I was supposed to be president after Bernie finished his term, but he was on the road a great deal, so I just stepped up my term and took on the day-to-day duties of the office. Bernie was flying around the country uplifting and inspiring thousands with his powerful healing messages, so I figured that this was the least I could do. Because I assumed that Bernie was busy and not interested, I took the liberty of editing a piece he had written for the newsletter. And I didn't run the edits by him. As it turned out, he wasn't happy at all with what I had done. But I knew what was necessary. I called him and said, "I am 100 percent responsible for those edits. No one else." And with that, he told me that he now trusted me more than ever. Because I hadn't tried to hide behind anyone else and pretend that I wasn't responsible.

Over the years I have found that this same honesty has served me over and over again. And it gets easier and easier. And as my brother John says, "I always tell the truth. Then I don't have to remember what I said."

Become Shame Resilient

In addition to letting your shame go and taking responsibility for your story, you have to address shame in life as it comes your way. In essence, you have to become shame resilient so you don't take on additional pain that eats away at your self-worth.

Since we live in a shaming society, we need to spot the shaming and dissolve it with love whenever we see it—both in our own lives and in the lives of those around us. The other day I posted a picture of my good friend Noah Levy and me at a book signing. In front of us were three bottles of a big brand-name water. Someone immediately posted: "I can't believe you are drinking that. It's poison." Clearly there were a couple of water activists in my audience. They suggested that I watch the documentary *Tapped*, so I could see everything I was doing wrong. My first response was to get defensive. I hadn't brought the water. The event space had put it there. I wasn't bad. But I stopped myself. You see, the thing is, I just wanted to post a nice thank-you to the people who came to my book signing. Not get into a harangue about bottled water.

Here's how I used to handle this kind of situation, especially on social media. I'd use it as an opportunity to educate people about the importance of not shaming. I would say something like, "This is a shame-free zone. You are welcome to share your opinion. But when you call me names, you are shaming me. And, believe it or not, that harms you. But when I stand up for myself, my immunity actually improves. (This is based on the scientific work of Dr. Mario Martinez.) So—please don't criticize or shame me or anyone else here on this page." Then I would set a boundary. If someone persisted in shaming, me, I'd press "ban user" and remove them from my page. The problem was that calling out someone on their behavior just never worked. And it never seemed to heal the situation in any way.

Then I learned another approach from spiritual teacher Matt Kahn that feels much better. Matt says he just "likes" all the comments on his Facebook page—no matter what they say. Then he sends Divine Love to anyone who criticizes and victimizes other people. He does this because he says these people are simply treating others the way they have been treated. When you acknowledge (to yourself) that that person is in pain and that's why they're acting the way they are acting, you help break the pattern of victim/victimizer. There is a level at which the other person will feel this.

You can also give them a compliment or send a blessing. That will really loosen the death grip of their ego.

Don't get me wrong here. I'm not suggesting you stay in an abusive relationship in which someone (even on social media) is routinely critical and victimizing. When someone gets really nasty, I still press "ban user."

But acknowledging the pain of another and sending love (whether in person or on social media) will stop you from feeling dominated by their harshness. It will also stop you from lowering your vibration to match theirs. That's what emotionally sensitive people (like you and me) tend to do when confronted with the confident and dominating ego of another. Instead, just rise in love, with confidence and conviction that the light always wins. Nothing breaks the hold of the ego faster than loving what arises, without shame or blame or righteousness.

So the next time someone tries to shame you, do something really radical. Just say, "Thank you." Then take it one step further. Compliment the person or bless them. From your heart. Then care for the part of yourself that was shamed. Say the following out loud in the mirror, gazing lovingly into your own eyes: "You are my beloved child, in whom I am well pleased."

What to Do When Blamed or Shamed

When you are blamed for something, whether it is justified or not, you feel shame or anger. The first thing to do is stop. Don't defend yourself. Simply scan your body. Where do you feel the blame? Breathe deeply into that spot. Feel the feeling of shame, blame, or anger, and then love the part of you that feels it. Understand that this part of you is who has just shown up to be loved. That alone can work wonders. That hurt, misunderstood child is actually receiving your love and attention. Great. Then take action.

Let's imagine that you were blamed for forgetting to pick up milk at the store. In this instance, ask yourself if the blame is justified. Did you say you would pick up that milk and then not do it?

- If the blame is justified, be accountable. Take responsibility. If you said that you'd pick up milk, admit that you messed up and then go get that milk.

- If the blame isn't justified, try to figure out the lesson in the blame. For example, if your wife simply mentioned that you were running low on milk but didn't ask you to get any, you can't be expected to pick up the milk. Very often we repeat childhood patterns in order to learn what our needs are—and to heal the wounds of childhood and learn our Soul lessons. If your father expected things from you without expressing what those things were, and you got in trouble because you didn't fulfill his expectations, you are likely to marry someone who works in the same way. The minute you see this pattern and love the part of yourself that feels blamed, you begin to build your self-esteem. Your inner child begins to feel worthy. And after a while, you will be unable to continue accepting blame for something that you can't possibly fix in your partner. You also have the opportunity to talk to your partner about your need to have things expressed clearly. Just don't go all righteous. Give them the benefit of the doubt.

From Survivor to Thriver

The power of releasing shame and stepping out of the powerlessness of the ego roles can be seen in what a lot of people refer to as miracles—complete remission from many different types of terminal cancers. Dr. Kelly Turner was a graduate student when she became interested in these phenomena. She noted that there were more than 1,000 well-documented cases of this nature listed on PubMed, an online database of peer-reviewed medical studies. When she began to read the case reports, she was stunned to see that on every one of them, the cause of the remission was listed as "unknown." So she made it her business to track down some of these people and find out what they had actually done to turn their conditions around. The end result is her book *Radical Remission: Surviving Cancer Against All Odds*. In it, she identified nine things that the survivors of cancer did to recover. Not everyone who gets over supposedly terminal cancer does every one of the nine. But most do at least a couple. The nine factors are the following:

1. Radically change their diet
2. Take control of their health
3. Follow their intuition
4. Use herbs and supplements
5. Release suppressed emotions
6. Increase positive emotions
7. Embrace social support
8. Deepen their spiritual connection
9. Have strong reasons to live

Please note that none of these super-thrivers stayed in the ego's roles. Not one. Instead they all found the power within themselves to life fully and well.

And interestingly enough, they don't identify with the label "cancer survivor." Nor do they wallow in the "myth of terminal uniqueness"—thinking that no one could possibly understand how wounded they are.

They've stopped using labels that limited their capacity for magnificence, such as having the word *survivor* attached to them. Labels like this put you in a group focused on an illness, making it harder to heal. They keep your focus on the problem rather than that bright, healthy future that lies ahead. Yes, there is a time and a place for support groups that help you "cope." But staying overly long in the "victim" or "survivor" mode is an invention of the ego.

Forgiveness: The Ultimate Cure for Blame and Guilt

Forgiveness is the final key that completely unravels the blame/guilt knot. Forgiveness is often misunderstood as condoning the bad things that were done to you. Or that you have done. That's not forgiveness. Forgiveness means no longer letting your past be your reason for not thriving in the present. Dr. Mario Martinez calls forgiveness "freedom from self-entrapment."

When I was going through my divorce, my first thought was that I had ruined my daughters' lives. But in time, I realized that by following the dictates of my Soul, I actually modeled something quite different for my children. I showed them that my life and my happiness (and therefore theirs too) actually mattered. And that staying overly long in a substandard situation was just a bad idea.

When we know better we do better. Beating ourselves up for what we didn't know in the past just keeps us stuck in blame and guilt. And that can fester for years.

Every single one of us has something in our past that requires forgiveness. And the very hardest person to forgive is ourselves. So let yourself off the hook, and begin by loving the part of yourself that feels unworthy and unforgivable.

Similar to releasing shame, forgiving yourself starts with acknowledging that which needs to be forgiven, and then asking for forgiveness. From yourself. From the Divine. From the universe. Do a Change Me Prayer: "Divine Beloved, please lift the burden of blame from my heart and from my life. Please remove my guilt and shame. And please change me into someone who feels worthy and whole. Change me into someone who feels totally and completely forgiven and free." In addition to asking the Divine for help, I also suggest that you simply help yourself. Say out loud: "I now release myself from the burden of guilt and shame."

Forgiving yourself also means extending love to yourself and meeting your own needs. The late Marshall Rosenberg, author of *Nonviolent Communication*, spent a lifetime teaching people how to get their needs met through nonviolent communication. He pointed out that every emotion we have indicates a need we have.

I remember the first time I did an exercise using Rosenberg's "needs" and "emotions" inventory. The group split into smaller groups of three. One person told a story from his or her life. The other two people listened for the emotion and the needs the emotions signified. We did this by looking at a series of single emotions written on small cards laid out in front of us—for example, anger, sadness, bitterness, irritability, joy, and happiness. As we listened, we'd hold up a card and ask the speaker if this was what he was feeling. Are you feeling anger? Sadness? Frustration? Once the emotions were validated, we'd then look at the needs cards (food, rest, appreciation, acknowledgment, touch, and so on) and hold up the card with the particular needs we felt we were hearing as we listened to the story. Our job was to reflect the unmet need that the emotions signified to the person telling the story.

This experience was a revelation for me. And a most powerful way of having my emotions and needs validated within community. It was the very first time that I ever experienced my needs as being legitimate and not something to deny or try not to have. Before that, I had judged my own needs (and emotions) as wrong or bad. Or something that I should somehow get over. That if I had been a more mature or developed human, I wouldn't have them. Talk about a no-win belief system! You can find the needs and emotions inventory at www.cnvc.org. It's well worth a look.

Having learned that our emotions signify legitimate needs, I was thrilled to learn of the five A's put forth by David Richo in his book *How to Be an Adult in Relationships: The Five Keys to Mindful Loving.* Those five A's are:

- Attention
- Appreciation
- Approval
- Affection
- Allowing

While the first four A's are pretty self-explanatory, *allowing* requires a bit of explanation. By this, Richo means that we must be allowed to follow the dictates of our Souls without having interference from others about what they think we "should" do.

These five A's are necessary to build our essential selves as children, and they are also necessary for happiness and fulfillment in our adult love relationships—and beyond. They apply to our relationships with ourselves, with the Divine, and with every other person on the planet. Luckily, we can give ourselves these five aspects of love, and by doing so, we help ourselves heal and forgive our past indiscretions. The five A's are what we all needed as babies and young children, but they are also the requirements of adult intimacy—in our relations with ourselves and those around us. Richo writes, "In the splendid economy of human and spiritual development, the same keys open all our evolutionary doors."

On Being Vulnerable

Releasing shame and stepping out of our ego roles helps develop connection and intimacy, the currency of a meaningful life. But if you're looking for the superfood of connection, look no further than vulnerability. Despite everything you may have been told about keeping a stiff upper lip or never letting them see you sweat, vulnerability is actually a superpower when it is used consciously and with a well-developed sense of self. Vulnerability is often misunderstood in our culture because it's associated with weakness, especially for men. The word itself means "capable of or susceptible to being hurt—as by a weapon. Or open to moral attack, criticism, or manipulation." No wonder we're taught to protect ourselves so zealously.

But vulnerability is actually about finding the strength within to allow your full humanity to be seen and touched by others—warts and all. Our vulnerability is endearing. It makes us human. In her groundbreaking TED talk on the power of vulnerability, which has now been seen by more than 26 million people, Brené Brown reminds us that connection—the ability to feel connected—is why we're here on this earth. Being vulnerable is part of feeling connected. It's what gives purpose and meaning to our lives. When we're willing to risk being vulnerable and fully human, we open to our humanity and our Divinity simultaneously. We know we belong. And we feel deeply worthy of the best that life has to offer.

So why is it so hard to be vulnerable? It all comes back to the ego protecting us from the pain of shame. But if you can step past this, life can become so much more full.

Several years after my divorce, a friend was visiting and I was being critical of my former husband. My friend told me that if I ever expected to have love in my life again, I had better get over my bitterness and anger. She suggested that I write him a love letter—telling him everything that I had loved about him. Knowing she was right, I got right on it. And on a full-moon night in January of that year—the very month our marriage had ended so abruptly several years before, I put on some soulful music, lit a candle, and came up writing (see the proprioceptive writing section on page 71).

All my love for this man came flooding back as I wrote about how much I had loved our courtship in medical school, how delighted I was to learn surgical knot tying from him. How much fun it was to scrub into surgical cases with someone I was so over the moon in love with. (He was my surgical intern when I was a med student. Very romantic.) And how grateful I was to have had him as a husband during the difficult years of residency and as the father of our two daughters. I was amazed at the flood of tears that were released.

And then I took it a step further. I read the letter out loud to him over the phone. It was right around Valentine's Day. He was remarried by this time, had had another child, and was living abroad. But in that moment between us, when I read him the letter, time simply stood still. There was nothing but love. We were in two different countries—with an ocean between us—but at that moment, we were two immortal Souls, unburdened by our egos and personalities. Just remembering the love—all of which was still there.

I was deeply moved and healed by doing this. And I highly recommend doing something similar in your life if there is someone you are still holding in resentment, bitterness, or anger. At the very least, write the letter. You don't have to read it to them or send it. You can burn it. But trust me, their Soul will feel it. And it doesn't need to be a love letter. It can be a diatribe of fury and release if it needs to be.

More recently, I did something like this with another man whom I had loved but with whom it didn't work out. And no matter what I did, I couldn't seem to get over him. I needed completion with this relationship. So I asked him to come to my house because there was something I needed to tell him. This was not for him; it was a gift for me. I asked him if he would please give me the gift of his presence and that he needn't do anything except listen. Then, with my full vulnerability flag flying, I sat him down at my kitchen table and proceeded to tell him that I had always loved him. That I still loved him. And that because life is short, I didn't want him to think that I was angry with him for the way things turned out. That I totally forgave him—and myself—for all of it. Even for the way it ended. When I was done, I hugged him. By the next day, I swear that the heaviness in my heart that had been there for the past several years was finally gone. And I was free. At last. And I haven't seen or talked to him since that night.

That is the power of vulnerability. You risk baring your Soul and wearing your heart on your sleeve. You open yourself up to criticism and ridicule. And in the end, you find that that doesn't matter at all. Because your Divine self can't be touched by any of that. You find, much to your surprise, that vulnerability is big medicine. Big, powerful medicine. The truth that sets you free, lightens your heart, and heals your world.

CHAPTER 9

Your Body, Your Temple

The thin red jellies within you or within me,
the bones and the marrow in the bones,
The exquisite realization of health;
O I say these are not the parts and poems
of the body only, but of the soul,
O I say now these are the soul!

— WALT WHITMAN

I think we've established by now that you are a Soul. You are *not* your body. But you do *have* a body. And it is your job to take care of that body until you leave it. The same way you take care of your house or your car. This is *your* responsibility—it doesn't belong to your doctor, your spouse, or your mother. It's that simple.

Taking care of your body means, first and foremost, having a healthy belief system about what's possible physically—especially as you move through time. Then you must engage in the physical activities necessary to maintain your physical self.

Beliefs about Your Body and Your Health

Optimal care of your body begins with your beliefs. It's important to know that your body was designed for health, vitality, and well-being for your entire life. Most people believe, however, that their bodies are destined to deteriorate with each passing year after about the age of 25. I've heard 32-year-olds complain about their bad backs and how their bodies are betraying them because of their age. Our bodies don't betray us. And they needn't deteriorate with every passing year. This is just a popular cultural belief system that is so common that when you look around you see it everywhere. But when you begin to change your beliefs about what's possible with your health and physical body, regardless of your age, you'll begin to experience positive changes more quickly than you believed were possible. Studies have shown, for example, that you can greatly improve muscle strength and mobility in people over 90 through weight training.

I wrote a whole book on how to identify and transform the adverse beliefs that many people have about what happens to their bodies as they grow older. It's called *Goddesses Never Age: The Secret Prescription for Radiance, Vitality, and Well-Being*. The number one message of that book is that your beliefs are more powerful than your genes. That's right. Your beliefs are, hands down, the most important factor that determines what happens to your body and your health. We covered this earlier when we talked about the power of thoughts and feelings, but I want to look at it again from a very physical perspective. Here's how thoughts affect your health.

As you know, every thought you think is accompanied by biochemical signals that move throughout your body. Serotonin, dopamine, and epinephrine are neurotransmitters that affect all areas of your body, and their production is based on what you think and feel. Stressful thoughts filled with anger, fear, or sadness increase stress-hormone levels in your body, which ultimately leads to cellular inflammation—the root cause of osteoporosis, depression, diabetes, heart disease, arthritis, and cancer.

But this isn't the only way thoughts affect our health. They can literally determine which genes are expressed. The genes in the DNA of a cell are regulated by swarms of molecules—so-called epigenetic factors. These molecules can respond to environmental influences by silencing some genes and activating others as needed.

Connecting Our Minds and Bodies

The power of thoughts on health was famously demonstrated by mindfulness pioneer Ellen Langer back in the 1990s. Langer took two groups of men, ranging in age from 70 to 87, and sequestered them away from their daily lives for about 10 days. Both groups went through an initial battery of tests to determine baseline hearing, eyesight, cardiac output, pulmonary function, blood pressure, weight, and visual appearance.

One group was instructed to simply go about their days as usual. The other group was instructed to live as though they were in their prime. Pictures of them at their "prime" (between the ages of 40 and 50) were posted on the walls. There were magazines from that earlier time available. And television shows from that time frame as well.

At the end of the 10 days, all of the baseline testing was repeated. Every parameter in the men who lived as if they were in their prime had improved. Their cardiac output was better, pulmonary functions were healthier—all of those things we think deteriorate with age had actually improved. Moreover, they all looked 10 years younger. A game of touch football even broke out among the group of men who were living "in their prime." The control group didn't have any improvement at all. Dr. Langer has since done many other experiments that prove how powerful our beliefs are on our physical functioning. You can read about them in her book *Counterclockwise*.

The most powerful demonstration of how beliefs affect our physical bodies comes from the research of Dr. Mario Martinez—and his work with stigmata—the wounds that show up on those who have a deep belief in and identification with the wounds Jesus suffered during the crucifixion.

Stigmata are painful physical wounds on the body that are symbolic of the suffering of Jesus. Dr. Martinez, with the cooperation of the Vatican, has studied people with stigmata. Some are frauds. And some are genuine. Padre Pio is one of the most famous people studied. One woman in particular, in Mexico City, had a very painful cross on her forehead. It bled daily. And when people came to her for healing, they were healed. Dr. Martinez was sent to study her. He cultured the wounds on her forehead and found that they were sterile. No bacteria. No infection. And absolutely no evidence of her wounds being self-inflicted. They were indeed a physical manifestation of her beliefs.

He asked her if she wanted relief for her suffering. She did. And together the two of them worked on the belief system in her body that had led to the wounds. Her forehead healed. But then people who came to her no longer got better. No stigmata, no healing. And so she and Dr. Martinez devised a workable compromise. She was able to get the cross on her forehead to decrease in depth, pain, and bleeding so that it was only about 20 percent of what it had been before. Her suffering decreased greatly—but didn't disappear. Her community of believers was still able to see the wound and thus heal.

This experience was one of many that led Dr. Martinez to create the Biocognitive Science Institute—the science that studies the profound connection between our beliefs and our physical health.

We all have familial and cultural beliefs handed down to us about our health, such as "Don't pick that up and eat it. It's got germs on it and you'll get sick." Or "I've been exposed to the flu. I catch everything that's going around the office. I know I'm going to get sick." Or "At my age I'm too old to [blank]." Beliefs have profound biochemical effects that actually change how our genes get expressed. The science of epigenetics has proven that your body responds to your environment, including your diet, thoughts, activity, and emotions. Since a belief is simply a thought that we keep on thinking, it can be changed. And our health can improve as a result.

Your Fascia: Where Beliefs Live in Your Connective Tissue

While the process of biochemical changes based on thought has started to gain widespread acceptance, there's another system of communication and information in the body that has been largely overlooked. And that is the network of connective tissue—known as fascia—that runs throughout the body. It connects the skin to the muscles, encases and runs throughout all the muscles, and also connects the muscles to the bones and to every organ in the body in one continuous, uninterrupted sheath. When you take the skin off a chicken, you are peeling away the fascial layers that connect that skin to the underlying muscle.

Because all the fascia is connected, what happens in one area of the body actually affects the fascia in all areas of the body. Once you realize this, you realize how limited medical specialties can be when they don't take into account the inherent wholeness of the body systems.

Our fascial network is a secondary nervous system that doesn't have pain fibers. Instead it acts like a crystalline electrical transmission system sending information throughout the body very rapidly. Acupuncture meridians run in this system, and when acupuncture needles are placed at specific points along those meridians, there are measurable effects in the organs associated with the specific points. Think about your feet. Your fascia begins at your feet and runs throughout your body up through your scalp—all as one piece. When you get a foot reflexology treatment or someone gives you a good foot rub, it's often so relaxing that you can't think. You might even go to sleep. That's because the stimulation of the fascia on your feet—where all the meridians of the body originate to some extent—affects every organ in your entire body, including your brain. In a good way. Of course this is also why when your feet hurt, everything else seems to hurt too.

Connective tissue in the body can become dense, scarred, and thickened as a result of physical, emotional, or mental stress. Stress leads to inflammation, then agglutination and thickening of connective tissue as the fibers stick together. Over time the body accumulates dense, scarred fascia in muscles and joints, which eventually leads to pain and a limited range of motion— and the halted, shuffling gait that we associate with being old. But it isn't just physical movement that is impeded. The area affected by scarring no longer enjoys a free flow of information, sensation, or blood supply. It becomes walled off from the rest of the body. The possibilities that we were born with for full movement and physical, emotional, and spiritual expression also become diminished over time.

Bob Cooley, who discovered a form of fascial stretching called Resistance Flexibility, was hit by a car going 80 miles an hour when he was 28 years old. (Talk about a rough Saturn Return!) His pelvis was fractured, his left leg was mangled, his shoulder was dislocated, and his left upper arm was ripped apart. He also sustained a head injury and went in and out of consciousness for a time. As you can imagine, he was left with difficulty walking and in constant pain.

Through self-experimentation, Bob, who had run a dance company and already specialized in biomechanics, discovered that muscles naturally contract when you stretch them. When he tensed his muscles and stretched them at the same time—just the way a dog or cat tenses and stretches when they get up from lying down—he could increase his range of movement. He could also decrease his pain. He eventually discovered stretches for each of the organ systems—stretches that mimicked the ancient yoga asanas (postures) and followed the principles of traditional Chinese medicine. Those stretches also helped him remove dense fascia and scar tissue from his muscles. He was able to not only restore normal function to his joints and muscles but also improve his digestion, lung capacity, thinking skills, and overall health. His health and mind became better after the accident than before. Though I had long known about the mind-body connection, it was from Bob and his trainers that I learned that that connection actually lives in our fascia. The unity of body, mind, emotions, and Spirit can be shown in the physical body. It's not just some New Age idea.

Through fascial stretching I discovered how profoundly our childhood beliefs and wounds shape how we inhabit and move in our physical bodies. This process was articulated very poetically by the late Isadora Duncan, a famous dancer:

> Very little is known in our day of the magic which resides in movement, and the potency of certain gestures. The number of physical movements that most people make through life is extremely limited. Having stifled and disciplined their movements in the first stages of childhood, they resort to a set of habits, seldom varied. So too, their mental activities respond to set formulas, often repeated. With this repetition of physical and mental movements, they limit their expression until they become like actors who each night play the same role.

By stretching and "reading" my fascia, Bob was able to determine that I had abandoned myself to try to heal my mother after the death of my baby sister. This childhood trauma, which I had not been aware of consciously, is what led me to become an ob/gyn and try to save so many other mothers and babies. The emotional trauma of this, and the fact that my mother, bless her, did not know how to love me (she did other things well) had left dense fascia around my heart—my "weak link," as Bob called it. By having the dense fascia in my heart meridian shredded and freed up, I found myself feeling much more comfortable in my own skin. As Bob said, "When you first came here, you looked so unlovable." He pointed out the inward turning of my shoulders, which advertised to the world that I felt unlovable. True then. No longer true. The other perk of having my heart meridian fascia shredded was the fact that I no longer feel so compelled to rescue people. A huge relief. There is so much more joy and freedom of movement in my life.

You've probably noticed that children tend to walk like their parents. And move like them. This isn't because of genetics. It's because, to fit in, we tend to imitate what we see around us. We shut down our full range of activities when we're repeatedly told to keep our voices down or sit still. Over time, this kind of conditioning greatly limits what our physical bodies are capable of experiencing. It also lays down dense fascia patterns that restrict movement.

But once you start to learn how to shred the dense fascia that holds old beliefs and behaviors in place, then you, quite literally, can be reborn. At any age.

Cleaning Up Your Fascia

There are many ways to address dense fascia, including yoga, Pilates, and acupuncture. Other types of body work, including Rolfing, Yamuna ball rolling, and the MELT method also address fascia. Even just running the bottom of your foot over a tennis ball while sitting at a desk begins to reshape your fascia. My sister completely "cured" her frozen shoulder by rolling the back of her shoulder muscles over a tennis ball while leaning against a wall with the ball between her and the wall. It took a couple of weeks. But she now has free range of movement. You can find some good introductory videos on most of these techniques if you go to YouTube. Anything that stretches you, working with your flexibility, can help. John Barnes's Myofascial Release Approach has also assisted many individuals. John has trained practitioners throughout the world in his unique approach.

While all these methods are good, the fastest and most advanced process I've used to remodel my own fascia is the system first discovered by Bob Cooley. The stretches that are a part of this can assist anyone in remodeling their fascia as well as opening up new patterns of emotional and spiritual well-being. There are a number of YouTube videos available that show the stretches; Google "Resistance Flexibility" to find them. You can also learn more at www.BendableBody.com. Many have incorporated the principles of engaging the muscles while stretching them into yoga classes and other activities. Remember: Watch a cat or dog get up from a nap. Or notice how in the morning you stretch your arms over your head and tense your neck and face and shoulders while yawning. This is what resistance stretching is. If at all possible, I recommend getting assisted with your stretching. Ongoing workshops are also available in many locations throughout the United States so that you can work directly with a trainer skilled in the method.

Don't Just Sit There: Make Gravity Work for You

Regular movement—every day—is absolutely crucial for sustainable health and happiness. The late Paul Dudley White, M.D., the founder of the American Heart Association and the father of modern cardiology, knew this very well. I remember reading about him when I was a teenager and loving the line where he said he had two doctors: his right leg and his left leg! He rode his bike along the Charles River every day of his life. And also walked regularly.

Dr. Joan Vernikos, author of *Sitting Kills, Moving Heals*, was the chief of NASA's life-sciences division when John Glenn, the famous *Apollo* astronaut with "the right stuff," wanted to go back into space at the age of 77. Vernikos had no idea if that was safe or not, as no one that old had ever gone into space. But Glenn kept up the same training pace as the other much younger astronauts, so he was permitted to go on the shuttle *Discovery* with his colleagues. He performed his duties with ease, and when he came back to Earth, he was no worse for wear than the other astronauts. But all of them, regardless of age, suffered from the effects of weightlessness for a couple of weeks. As Vernikos pointed out, these effects don't make the news. The effects of weightlessness include loss of balance, decreased cardiac output, decreased bone density, and loss of muscle mass—the same adverse effects Vernikos had seen and studied in perfectly healthy 20-year-old men who were confined to bed for several weeks to study the effects of inactivity on their bodies.

Vernikos's observations led her to the conclusion that weightlessness—not moving the body through the gravitational field of the earth regularly—was the cause of the deterioration we call "aging." Whether one is weightless from being in a gravity-free environment such as space, from lying in bed, or from prolonged sitting—the effect is the same.

The effects of inactivity and not moving the body through gravity are so adverse that we're now calling sitting the "new smoking." Prolonged sitting (more than six hours a day) increases your risk of just about everything including heart attack, stroke, diabetes, obesity, and cancer. In fact, even if you exercise regularly, prolonged sitting cancels out a lot of the good effects. It also begins to lay down dense fascia in the hip joints, a process that can start in your 20s. Long before you notice a hip problem, the inevitable first step in eventual decline begins if you don't start moving.

Remember, all of this happens because you're not moving regularly against gravity. Every time you move your body through gravity—even something as simple as bouncing up and down a bit on the balls of your feet—your body goes through thousands of minute physiologic changes in blood pressure, fluid exchange, hormone secretion, and stresses on bones and joints that help ensure health.

Standing all day is not the answer either. Same problem. The answer is moving your body through the gravitational field of the earth. Regularly. That means getting up about six times per hour if you sit at a desk. Just standing up and then sitting down again is enough to make a big difference. But if you can it's always best to add in something more, like some stretching or knee bends. Or you can stand while working on your computer—and then do squats regularly. Or you can bounce on the balls of your feet regularly. Or walk around a bit every 15 minutes. I sit on a yoga ball while I'm working on my computer—and bounce regularly. Bottom line: We are not meant to be weightless. We are designed to move through space. Rebound trampolines are perfect for this. You might consider getting one and bouncing on it while watching television. Another great option is bouncing on a big yoga ball while sitting at your computer. It's fun. And it will keep you joyfully moving through space!

Practicing Balance

There's a big debate in medicine that goes like this: Did she break her hip and then fall? Or did her fall create the break in the hip? It doesn't matter which it is; the problem is that about 50 percent of people who break their hips will never walk again. And that doesn't need to happen if you learn how to maintain your balance.

Remember those astronauts who lost their balance from being weightless? Another part of the problem is that they didn't have a horizon to orient to. But you do. So you can easily practice and greatly improve you balance. Just do this:

1. Take off your shoes.

2. Stand on one foot for as long as you can.

3. Now close your eyes.

4. Change feet and stand for as long as you can.

Did you find that you needed to put the other foot down for balance almost immediately when you closed your eyes? When I first started to do this, I was horrified that I lost my balance as soon as I closed my eyes. So I kept practicing, at least three or four times a day. I did it when waiting in line at the grocery store. Standing at the sink brushing my teeth. Standing at the stove cooking dinner. And here's what I found: Within two weeks, I was able to easily stand for 30 seconds or longer on one foot with my eyes closed. That's how fast the vestibular system, which is responsible for balance, heals itself.

So do yourself a favor: Make practicing balance a regular part of your daily routine. And then if you slip on something, chances are really good that you'll easily maintain your footing. This is real preventive medicine.

Enjoy Regular Movement

While making sure we move through gravity regularly will prevent all sorts of ailments associated with getting older, we have to remember that our bodies were designed to move even more than that. Climbing trees, running, crawling, dancing—all of these activities will not only maintain your physical health, they will improve it.

So many people opt out of movement because they believe that it's arduous. They don't want to exercise. They can't play sports. They're not coordinated. I blame these perceptions of movement on the physical education systems in schools that have focused for far too long on sports skills. And on the culture of sports in general. Sports are just fine if that's what you like. But there is so much more to physical activity than simply interacting with a ball—whether hitting it, kicking it, or running with it. If you adore golf and tennis, by all means, keep playing. I have many friends on adult hockey teams. Male and female. They love it. And it keeps them active. But not all of us were designed for team sports. My mother has spent a lifetime skiing. My sister just took up surfing. My two sisters-in-law train and ride horses.

I'm finally fulfilling a childhood desire to dance, something that was quashed when the only dance teacher in my small town left—the very week that my tap shoes came in the mail. But since the Soul knows no timeline, it's never too late. And now my tap shoes have been traded in for tango shoes.

To live well you have to move. Pure and simple. So find a way you like to move—alone or with a group. And begin. Or continue. And don't ever stop.

Your Feet: Your Foundation

Now let's talk about your feet. I've already mentioned that the soles of your feet contain a map of every organ system in your body. The health of your feet and your toes are a direct reflection of the health of your entire body. Try this: Take off your shoes if you're wearing any. Now spread your toes out as wide as you can. You should be able to see spaces between each of your toes. If those spaces aren't there, you need some footwork. There's a product called Yoga Toes that you can insert between your toes in order to stretch the fascia between them and loosen them up. You can also grab your foot with the opposite hand and thread your fingers into the spaces between your toes—attempting to get the entire length of your finger in between each one. Once you have them there, rotate the front of your foot in circles. When I was first shown this exercise by my Pilates teacher, Hope Matthews, the pain was unbelievable. But I kept at it. And now I can easily interdigitate my fingers with my toes on both sides. And I do this often—in the bathtub—especially after a night of tango dancing.

Hope has a series of foot exercises available via her website. These have transformed my feet. Check out www.sparhawkpilates.com. You can also find some YouTube videos on Pilates foot exercises.

We all need to free our feet from the tyranny of shoes on a regular basis. I realize that shoes can be gorgeous and sexy fashion statements. I have an entire tango shoe "altar" dedicated to the perfection of a beautiful shoe. However, my time in tango shoes—or any high heels—is strictly limited. I'm in them for no more than two hours at a time. Maybe once or twice a week, max. That's *it*! As Katy Bowman points out so masterfully in her book *Whole Body Barefoot*, shoes are, quite literally, casts for the feet. They severely limit your ability to use all the muscles and joints in your feet. They kind of freeze all that movement into place. And then, over time, you develop all kinds of problems that are completely preventable. Those problems include plantar fasciitis, hammer toes, bunions, corns, and the inability to walk barefoot in sand. I've known dozens of people who've been given orthotics to help their feet. And then they end up with feet that are so deconditioned and weak that they can no longer walk without the orthotics. The path to healthy, happy feet is this: Keep your feet stimulated and strong.

Loving Your Feet

Keeping your feet in tiptop shape is easy. You just have to make sure they experience all sorts of different kinds of movement. So walk barefoot regularly, especially outside whenever possible. Consider buying a pebble mat. This uneven surface stimulates the entire sole of the foot—and your entire body. Keep a tennis ball handy. Roll your foot over it regularly. Exercise your feet by pulling a towel toward you with your toes curling in and grasping it. Then extend the towel back out in the opposite direction by spreading your toes and pushing it away. Anyone can do these simple exercises, and you'll be amazed at how fast your feet respond.

Remember also that hip and knee problems very often begin with your feet and the wrong shoes. And quite frankly, all shoes, other than the minimal footwear kind, are the wrong shoes. Remember when mothers were taught that their babies required shoes when starting to walk? Theoretically they needed them for support. But the minute you put a shoe on a young child, the child loses the connection to earth and begins to walk like Frankenstein's monster—instead of running lightly on his or her toes. You've seen this, I know. It's happened to far too many of us.

So after strengthening your feet, switch to minimal footwear. With no heel. A heel pushes your body forward and throws off the alignment of your entire body. Katy Bowman suggests that we think of fancy high heels as "dessert." They're okay occasionally. Not every day.

Shake It Out, Dance It Out, Cry It Out

We are born with the capacity to release the emotions that affect our body; it's naturally wired into all mammals, including humans. Do you remember the shaking I mentioned in Chapter 3? After a gazelle has run from a predator, it shakes. After a woman has delivered a baby, she shakes. Uncontrollably. This is because their bodies are releasing those intense emotions. Other ways to do this include tears and sound. Tears have toxins in them. And when they are shed, toxins get released. Movement, tears, and sound are like grappling hooks that go through the body and release chronic tension held in the nervous system, muscles, and fascia.

But the shaking doesn't start, and neither do the tears or the wailing, until you feel safe. Until you can afford to finally relax.

I have a good friend who suffered a major concussion when a heavy mast from a boat fell on his head. He's a strong guy, a skilled competitor, and a master of his craft of building boats. As you might imagine, taking a moment to shake and cry is simply not in his nature. But about six years after his head injury, he found himself breaking down and weeping uncontrollably during a medical examination in which he had to recount the details of the accident. This happened a couple of times. And he couldn't believe it. I reassured him that this is the body finally feeling safe enough to release the chronic tension in the cells.

It's imperative that you regularly create safe space in which to really relax and let go, whether that comes through crying, shaking, singing, or just dancing around.

Remember that the ego develops in childhood from an over-stimulated nervous system. The subconscious mind comes up with beliefs—many of which are passed down in families—in order to make sense of all the experiences the child is having. For instance, if a parent leaves the child to "cry it out" until the point where the child throws up from the stress, the child may, in response, encode the belief *I can't trust anyone to be there for me. I better rely on myself.* And that belief will be stored in the connective tissue, which may very well influence how that child looks and moves, and who she attracts later in her life.

It bears repeating that with all the new experiences and stimuli that a baby has to respond to, it becomes easier over time to hold tension in the body rather than take the trouble to get completely relaxed into a blissful state. This is because, once the baby is fully relaxed again, it is very jarring to be pulled out of it yet again. It's easier to just stay in a state of chronic tension. And holding on to that chronic tension is the beginning of losing our innate flexibility.

I've had the opportunity to watch how all this plays out with my baby granddaughter. Her mother (my daughter Kate) learned that sometimes babies just need to cry it out as a way to relieve accumulated tension—just like adults—but also as a way to communicate the need for more rest. (We all get cranky when we need more sleep, right?) When little Penelope needs to cry it out, her parents set a timer for about five minutes and hold her while she cries. And talk to her. After five minutes, they do whatever is necessary (rocking, bouncing, singing) to soothe the crying if it's still going on. Almost invariably—unless there has been a huge amount of new stimulus, such as a plane trip—the crying stops within five minutes and leads to a very contented and happy baby who falls asleep with ease. Because of this loving care, Penelope is a generally happy child.

I believe that the same thing is true for all of us, adults included. If we felt truly safe, had a place to cry it out when necessary, and could sleep when we needed to, then our fascia wouldn't get so dense and we wouldn't have the health problems we have.

Unshed tears and stifled cries build up in the body as pressure in the cells, which shows up as cellular inflammation. Many adults, when they first feel tears arising, stifle them almost immediately so that they can get back in control. This is what they learned in childhood. This is especially true for men who are socialized to never cry or admit vulnerability or weakness. What is far more helpful is this: When strong emotions arise, assess whether or not this is a safe place in which to shed them. Will you be supported if you let loose? If not, let your body know that you'll get back to it later. And then, when you have a free moment, find a safe spot and allow yourself to go all the way into your pain. Cry it out. Really wail. Lie still until the tears arise. And shake if your body feels the urge to do so. Go all the way down and in. You may at first feel that if you allow yourself to really release the unshed tears, you will never emerge from the pain. But here's what you'll find: The body has its own intelligence. Like a baby who is allowed to safely cry it out, your body knows how to cry it out as well. You'll often emerge looking 10 years younger. The pressure in your cells will have been released. You will emerge from your crying with a new level of joy and freedom. When you allow yourself the freedom to just cry it out when necessary, you are far less likely to build up dense fascia in your body that will restrict your movements.

It's a nice system, isn't it? Built-in detox. No batteries required. Give it a try next time you feel those tears arising and your throat closing. Slow, deep breathing helps a great deal also. Take 10 slow, deep breaths through your nose and out through your nose whenever you feel stressed or just would like to feel a bit of bliss. This can work wonders. Your body will be very grateful to you.

CHAPTER 10

Eat Well and Tend Your Inner Garden

*True health-care reform starts in
your kitchen, not in Washington.*

— ANONYMOUS

Though we are far more than what we eat, our bodies run best on the highest-grade fuel possible. When you pull up to a gas pump, there are three choices: regular, medium grade, and premium. All cars run best on premium. It burns better and leaves less residue. It's the same with your body.

What you eat contains the building blocks that become your tissues and organs. When I was doing my surgical training and in the operating room regularly, I was astounded by the variations in the quality of people's skin and tissue. Some had resilient, strong connective tissue. In others—even as young as 18—the tissue was so weak and of such poor quality that you could actually separate it with your fingers while making an abdominal incision or moving different organs out of the way. The healthy tissue required a scissors or knife to separate it. One of my professors called the weak stuff "taco tissue," meaning that it resulted mostly from a fast-food diet high in simple carbohydrates without enough fresh produce and protein.

When skilled body workers touch people to stretch their fascia or massage their muscles, the first thing they can tell is the quality of the individual's tissue. And the quality of that tissue is vastly improved by eating an organic, whole-food diet. Quality whole food—grown in soil with a high nutrient content—is vital not only for maintaining optimal health but also for recovering from illness. I like to say that eating whole organically grown food is like breast-feeding from Mother Earth herself. Just as there is no substitute for breast milk as the optimal food for babies, there is no substitute for food that is directly grown on the land or in the sea.

What Diet Is Best?

There is no shortage of books out there telling you what you should eat. The problem is that they often contain conflicting messages. For a couple of decades, the virtues of low-fat, vegan eating were extolled. Then there were and are the raw-food enthusiasts who say we should never subject our food to heat lest the enzymes be ruined. Now the pendulum has swung back. Fat is no longer the enemy that it has been made out to be for the past 40 years. The new enemy is refined sugar.

I've been on the front lines of the diet and nutrition movements for decades. I've witnessed how powerful food is as medicine. I've seen people experience dramatic healing by simply changing their diets. And I've personally tried every diet known to humanity—from low-fat vegan, to macrobiotic, to Atkins, to ketogenic. I was raised on organic foods and good supplements, long before it was popular. I've read nearly every health-food book, cookbook, and diet book ever written. And I've helped thousands of women become healthy, make peace with their weight, and learn to enjoy delicious food. Much of my interest in food and nutrition is, in addition to my role as a doctor, also the result of a decades-long battle with my weight—always thinking I was 10 to 20 pounds overweight. And I am far from alone in this.

The bottom line with diets is that one size doesn't fit all. Different diets work for different people. Some people thrive on low-fat, vegan diets; others gain weight on them or get depressed. So you have to experiment a bit to see what works for you. That said, there are a few tried-and-true rules for healthy eating that apply to everyone.

Rule 1: Follow the 80–20 Rule

If you're well, you want your diet to be mostly whole, natural foods, and mostly plants, 80 percent of the time. I'm talking vegetables, fruits, nuts, and legumes—preferably organic. Animal food should be a condiment. And when you do eat it, animal protein should come in the form of grass-fed dairy, free-range chickens, grass-fed beef, naturally raised pork, and wild game. Most people need a little animal protein to feel their best. Some don't do well with dairy products or eggs. Almost everyone would do well to limit grains.

The other 20 percent of the time, let yourself off the hook. Join the party and enjoy. Don't stress about what you're eating. Like when you step off a plane that didn't serve a thing, you're starving, and you can't pass up the first bite of something you can find. Even a Cinnabon. Don't beat yourself up for being human. You have thousands of years of evolution running through your veins, and the main thrust of that force is for you to survive—by eating the sweetest, fattiest food you can possibly find. The kind that will get you through a long winter or long period of starvation. Just don't do it all the time. You'll probably find, though, that as time goes on, you're not going to be tempted even a little by junk food. It will simply leave your experience.

Luckily, it's getting easier and easier to eat organic food because of farmers' markets, farm-to-table restaurants, and companies like Thrive market, which delivers deeply discounted organic packaged food right to your door—in record time. Since organic produce can be expensive, a good alternative is to check out the Environmental Working Group's Dirty Dozen and Clean Fifteen lists, which were created to give people insight on which vegetables are grown with the most and least pesticides and harmful chemicals. If you can't buy all organic produce, shop smart and opt to spend a bit more on organics for the items on the Dirty Dozen list. You can find the full list at www.ewg.org/foodnews.

When trying to eat healthy, planning is key. Stock your cupboards and fridge with good produce. Spend Sunday—or your day of choice—prepping food so it's easy to grab and go. You need to have good food easily available at all times, otherwise it becomes easier to get a takeout pizza, which breaks down into sugar very quickly (believe it or not) and is just not a good dietary staple. There are dozens of books that can help you do this. I recommend everything and anything by Kris Carr or by Mark Hyman. Both Anthony William's *Medical Medium* and David Ludwig's *Always Hungry?* have some great information. Also David Perlmutter's *The Grain Brain Cookbook* and William Davis's *Wheat Belly.* Joan Borysenko's *The PlantPlus Diet Solution* is a favorite of mine because it addresses the wide range of individual differences when it comes to diet. All of these books contain delicious recipes. Yes, there is conflicting material in them, but there is also a huge amount of overlap! They're great resources to get you started.

Enhancing Food with Love

When you're somewhere that serves foods you don't normally eat, you don't need to abstain from eating. You simply need to turn to love.

Accept your fast-food burger or fish sandwich or salad or fries, and before taking a bite, bless the food with the healing power of Divine Love. Say something like: "With my Spirit and the angels' help, I bring Divine Love into this food. I ask that it be rendered safe and healthy for me to eat. I ask for this according to the Creator's will." Then draw in your breath through your nose. Hold it for a couple of seconds. And then pulse it out through your nose.

The other way to charge suboptimal food with love is to realize the love that went into its preparation. If you're a guest at someone's house, the food they serve is often made in the spirit of love—even if it's not the gluten-free vegan fare you prefer. If you truly need to strictly follow a special diet, make sure to inform your hosts *before* you go. And do them the favor of bringing your own food. Do not expect your hosts to have gone out of their way to prepare a special meal for you. But if you're not sick and there is no risk to eating their food, here's what you do. Ask yourself the following: "Was the food prepared with love?" Chances are that it's loaded with the love and care of those who prepared it for you. These are the times when food really *is* love. So just enjoy it, knowing that the energy of love and care has imbued the food. And—because it can only help—bring Divine Love into the food. Here's the short way: "I bring Divine Love into this food." Now pulse your breath. You're done.

Rule 2: Avoid Addictive Food Additives

Most processed, packaged foods are loaded with highly addictive substances designed to make you eat too much. The biggest perpetrator of this is monosodium glutamate, or MSG. MSG is found in many processed foods and is called by many names (see the box on page 156), perhaps the most confusing of which is "natural flavorings." Eighty percent of all natural flavorings—even those found in foods at health-food stores—contain MSG. This is because the United States allows natural flavors to include protein hydrolysates, which can contain up to 20 percent MSG by weight. Don't trust something simply because it is labeled as "natural" or even "organic."

MSG in its many guises dramatically increases food cravings and binge eating because it is an excitotoxin that stimulates the brain to keep eating. In labs it's actually used to create obesity in mice. Sadly it does the same thing in humans. This substance also can cause headaches, sweating, rapid heartbeat, chest pain, nausea, and a number of other reactions.

MSG in Its Many Guises

If you see any of the following ingredients listed on the label of something you're considering buying, put it back on the shelf! It's got MSG—or a replacement ingredient that your body reacts to in the same way.

- monosodium glutamate

- glutamate

- hydrolyzed vegetable protein

- yeast extract

- gelatin

- protein hydrolysates

- natural flavorings

- Senomyx (an MSG replacer)

Virtually 100 percent of conventionally produced snack foods in the middle aisles of the grocery store are loaded with MSG. This is why you can't eat just one—and I'm not talking one piece here. You consume the entire bag—and then you want another one. Even though you know you'll feel awful the next day. Big Food knows this. And they know how to keep you hooked. Save yourself the trouble of trying to stop by not starting in the first place.

Another perpetrator in packaged foods is partially hydrogenated fats, which prolong shelf life dramatically. The problem is that all hydrogenated fats are chemically made in a lab and interfere with cell membrane and brain function. They are not found in nature, and they interfere with normal cellular function. They are also known carcinogens.

Other addictive and harmful food additives include the artificial sweeteners aspartame, sucralose, and saccharin. The list of illnesses that have been associated with consuming these substances is too long to give in full, but it includes conditions such as hyperactivity, seizures, headaches, panic attacks, hallucinations, nausea, diarrhea, and so many others. It's also possible that these sweeteners promote obesity and associated problems such as diabetes. They do this by messing with the balance of bacteria in your gut. Basically, it's bad stuff, so avoid it.

Because packaged foods can be so detrimental to your health, the best bet is to read labels. But there are also some rules of thumb that can help guide your buying:

- The saltier a processed food is, the more likely it is to contain MSG.

- The more processed a food is, the more likely it is to contain MSG. Virtually all conventional powdered soup mixes are loaded with MSG. Same with bouillon cubes.

- The more ingredients in a packaged food, the more likely MSG is present.

- If something is sweet but not heavy on calories, it is likely to have artificial sweeteners.

- Light, diet, and sugar-free foods likely contain artificial sweeteners.

- The longer the list of ingredients, the higher the chances that a food isn't good for you.

Rule 3: Get Smart about Gluten

Everywhere you look you find foods made with wheat. But wheat is not what it used to be. In his book *Wheat Belly*, cardiologist William Davis points out that the wheat we're eating today is a far cry from the wheat of 50 years ago; it has been genetically modified almost beyond recognition. Wheat, and most other gluten-containing grains, also contain a protein called gliadin—along with others—which is toxic to many cells in the body. When gliadin is ingested, some of it inevitably gets into the bloodstream. The immune system then marks it for destruction, but because gliadin is very much like thyroid tissue, that immune response can adversely affect the thyroid gland as well as the gliadin. This sets up an inflammatory response that destroys thyroid tissue. People with thyroid problems, including Graves' disease and Hashimoto's thyroiditis, should avoid gluten completely. Not just a little. Completely.

I have a good friend who has had a long history of hypothyroidism. She followed a diet plan with no gluten for a month and lost 20 pounds. She also felt fantastic. On a family vacation, she ate a muffin. And gained 10 pounds. Within two days. She has a Ph.D. in nutrition and is a nurse. She didn't make this up. That one muffin set her system back for months. She learned that she has zero tolerance for gluten. Many other people have found the same thing.

We used to think that gluten sensitivity was very rare, and we diagnosed it only in those with true celiac disease. But with all the changes in wheat and in our diets, and the vast amount of refined flour that is consumed daily by so many—in the form of pretzels, crackers, pasta, and bread—I'd say that the majority of people don't tolerate gluten well at all and should eliminate grains from their diets as much as possible. Doing so very often eliminates things such as joint pain, excess weight, sinus problems, and allergies of all kinds—and that's just for starters. Neurologist David Perlmutter has shown, unequivocally, how bad grains are for the brain. His groundbreaking book *Grain Brain* tells the whole story. Many people have completely cured their epilepsy by following a grain-free diet. Grain consumption is also associated with dementia down the road. Part of this is from the fact that grain products are rapidly converted into sugar. And we now know that Alzheimer's disease is actually type 3 diabetes. That's right—it's related to high blood sugar.

While you may be tempted to go out and get a test—because you just *love* bread and can't imagine giving it up—keep in mind that gluten intolerance isn't going to show up on standard medical testing. So don't waste your time or money trying to find out whether you're gluten intolerant. Trust me on this: Just eliminate all grains for two weeks. Then add some back and see what happens.

There are some gluten-free grains, like kamut and quinoa, that are delicious. Just use them in moderate amounts, not as staple foods. You can also enjoy pastas made with beans, such as organic black bean spaghetti. A whole new world of flavor and health opens up when you eliminate gluten.

However, a word of caution about gluten-free products. Responding to market pressure, many companies are now making gluten-free foods in which they substitute potato starch or tapioca for the wheat. I finally read the label on some gluten-free bread I was truly enjoying, which claimed to be made from millet and chia seeds. Here's what the label said: water, tapioca starch, brown rice flour, millet, egg whites, corn syrup, cane sugar syrup, potato starch, dry molasses, cornstarch, and a bunch of other chemicals. No wonder I liked it so much! It was kind of like eating candy. The bread was made primarily from sugar—or foods that quickly became sugar.

I now mostly stay away from gluten-free breads and baked goods of all kinds. Just like my bread, many of these foods are packed with sugar. So don't make the mistake of thinking that just because it's a gluten-free cookie it's good for you. It isn't. There are some healthy gluten-free options, but many of them aren't found at a regular grocery store. I have discovered a delicious locally baked bread to eat now and again. Check out these ingredients: unbleached white flour, water, stone ground rye flour, water, yeast, caraway seed, and salt. That's it. This is clearly the healthier choice all around.

Rule 4: Not All Sugar Is Bad

We are all born with a natural sweet tooth. Breast milk is essentially sugar water, with all kinds of amazing immune properties added in by Mother Nature. The same force of love that gave us our sweet tooth has also provided a healthy and natural way to satisfy our cravings: fruit. Take a moment and think about how symbolic that word is in everyday language: *The endeavor bore fruit. Be fruitful and multiply. The fruit of the womb.*

Yes, I know that there is sugar in fruit. But it's not the same as the concentrated refined sugar that's added to everything from soups to soft drinks, creating foods not found in nature. Fruit contains all kinds of antioxidant nutrients and fiber that are good for us. Anthony William points out that the sugar in fruit leaves our stomachs very quickly and goes to our cells to be burned as fuel.

In his book *Medical Medium*, Anthony has an entire eye-opening chapter on the health benefits of fruit. He also extols the virtues of—wait for it—potatoes. Not the "loaded" baked potatoes with sour cream, bacon bits, and butter. Just the nice out-of-the-ground potatoes found around the world, especially the small, organic red-skinned or multicolored ones. Until I heard Anthony's take on fruit and potatoes and their health benefits, I had been avoiding both—except for berries and an occasional apple—for years because of my concerns about sugar.

My intellectual knowledge about "all sugar is bad and makes you gain weight" was so ingrained that I was actually afraid to try the detox cleanse in Anthony's book. That cleanse is basically raw fruits and vegetables for 28 days. But I finally did a version of it, and it turned out to be very satisfying. I say that I did a version of it because I couldn't tolerate the coldness of that food during a Maine winter—so I just baked some potatoes, onions, and sweet potatoes for my evening meal and enjoyed this with a salad containing lots of greens dressed with a delicious avocado, orange juice, and cilantro dressing. Other than that potato, I ate raw all day. Each morning started with a smoothie of frozen wild Maine blueberries, bananas, peaches, organic strawberries or raspberries, apples, and maybe some spinach or barley green powder. And a couple of dates. With a splash of lemon juice.

I found this way of eating so satisfying and delicious that I didn't want to stop—and I haven't. I just add some occasional fish or chicken now. And dishes made with beans. All my former cravings for sugar, caffeine, baked goods, and grains just disappeared. I found that Anthony was right: When you let nature feed you the fruits she has chosen for you, your body says, "Yes. Thank you." My morning smoothies have now become a staple of my diet. They also get rave reviews when I serve them to my guests.

Now that you know that fruit is not your enemy, what about other sugars and sweeteners?

Some are okay. Some are not. A little honey or maple syrup now and again is okay. Also date sugar.

As for the noncaloric sweeteners, it's best to opt for a little stevia. Emphasis on *a little*.

Stevia is all natural, derived directly from the stevia plant, and has no adverse effects. Its sweet leaves have been used for centuries, and over the past decade or so, all kinds of products containing stevia have become available, including the soda known as Zevia, sweetened with Truvia, a stevia extract. It's also easy to grow in your own garden, which is a plus because you can control exactly how it's produced.

You may be asking why you have to stick with just a little of it if it's got so many benefits.

While discussing stevia with endocrinologist and obesity expert Dr. David Ludwig, author of *Always Hungry?: Conquer Cravings, Retrain Your Fat Cells and Lose Weight Permanently*, and his wife, whole-foods chef Dawn, I learned that in many individuals, the intense sweetness of stevia may be a culprit in preventing weight loss. Fat cells have "taste buds" on them as part of monitoring their environment. The mere taste of sweetness may increase insulin production, which signals fat cells to continue to store fat.

After I met with the Ludwigs, they suggested that I eliminate stevia—and all other sweeteners, including fruits—for two solid weeks so that my taste buds could reset. I realized that I was pretty addicted to sweetness, so this presented a challenge. To help me, they suggested that I add more healthy fats to my diet to increase satiety. I reluctantly agreed to say good-bye to sweets, and after two weeks, my taste buds had reset dramatically. Fruit tasted incredibly sweet to me—far sweeter than ever before. And my desire for stevia in my iced tea and coffee decreased dramatically. I now use only one or two drops—a lot less than the entire dropperful I used to use. And I am healthier as a result. Plus my sweet cravings are gone.

Other than the relatively healthy sweeteners listed earlier, it's best to avoid sugar because eating it spikes your blood sugar levels, which is bad for your health. The damage that comes from repeatedly spiking your blood sugar is slow and inexorable. It is the baseline cause of cellular inflammation, which contributes to all sorts of health problems.

Keep in mind that diets that are low in fat are rarely the kind that keep blood sugar stable. Diets that cut out fat are not very satisfying because they just don't taste good. In order to improve the taste and satisfaction, a lot of sugar is usually added. Just like with gluten-free products.

Blood Tests to Determine Your Blood Sugar Stability

To know how your blood sugar is doing, there are some simple blood tests I recommend.

- **Insulin response test (also called a glucose tolerance test):** This test measures your insulin levels one and two hours after consuming a standard glucose drink containing 75 grams of glucose. Your fasting insulin level will be the first thing that becomes abnormal when you've been following a diet that is spiking your blood sugar. This test will let you know that problems are brewing down the road if you continue eating as you have—long before your blood sugar levels show a risk for diabetes. It's an early warning.

  An alternative to this test is to buy a cheap glucometer at the drug store and test your own fasting glucose levels. It's easy. Test your blood sugar first thing in the morning. This is your fasting blood sugar level, and it should be between 70 and 85 milligrams per deciliter (mg/dL). Two hours after eating, test it again. It should not go above 120 mg/dL.

- **Hemoglobin A1C:** This test measures what your average blood sugar has been over the past six weeks by measuring the percentage of glycolated hemoglobin—the portion of your hemoglobin that has been "caramelized" with excess blood sugar. It should be 5.5 percent or below. Over 6.0 means you have diabetes. Your fasting standard glucose should be between 75 and 80 mg/dL. Anything higher is a risk factor.

If either of these tests comes back higher than normal, it's time to get serious about cutting down on the sugar in your diet.

Avoiding sugar can be hard because sugar is added to just about every packaged food out there—even foods you don't think of as sweet. Tomato sauce? Salad dressing? It can hide anywhere, so read labels and avoid products that list things like cane sugar or corn syrup. Check out the box below for many more names.

I've already suggested that you avoid grains. And that includes cereals. It's shocking to realize that all packaged and popular kids' cereals, including the "breakfast of champions," are pretty much nothing but sugar. They are as addictive as heroin. Maybe more so. So you need to educate yourself. Read labels. Avoid those foods in the future.

A Sugar by Any Other Name

Like MSG, sugar can go by many names. Here are some of the things you may see in ingredients lists—and any of these mean that sugar has been added:

- Anhydrous dextrose

- Brown sugar

- Cane juice

- Confectioners' powdered sugar

- Corn syrup

- Corn syrup solids

- Crystal dextrose

- Dextrose

- Evaporated corn sweetener

- Fructose

- Fruit juice concentrate

- Fruit nectar

- Glucose

- High-fructose corn syrup (HFCS)

- Honey

- Invert sugar

- Lactose

- Liquid fructose

- Malt syrup

- Maltose

- Maple syrup

- Molasses

- Nectars (e.g., peach nectar, pear nectar)

- Pancake syrup

- Raw sugar

- Sucrose

- Sugar

- Sugarcane juice

- White granulated sugar

The obesity epidemic in this country and worldwide has been driven largely by the huge amount of grains plus added sugar that are the mainstays of pretty much all prepackaged and processed foods—including fast foods. These foods are cheap, widespread, and deadly.

Rule 5: Know the Skinny on Fat

Fat is not the enemy it has been made out to be. We need healthy fats like coconut oil, avocado, seeds and nuts, and, yes, even butter. Saturated animal fat is okay too if the animals had a good life, were grass fed, and were not raised on antibiotics. Why do we need fat? Because our brains and the cover on all our nerves are mostly fat. If we don't supplement the fat in our bodies, it degrades and the organs that depend on it lose their ability to function well. This is why people on very low-fat diets tend to get depressed. It's like their wiring gets frayed.

When Dr. William Davis, the author of *Wheat Belly*, was on my Hay House radio show *Flourish!*, I asked him how he went from being an invasive cardiologist (doing angiograms and stents) to teaching about health. He started with his own personal experience, explaining that he went to a cardiology conference and listened to a well-known researcher extol the virtues of a low-fat, vegan diet. The talk was so impressive that he decided to follow this type of diet—and he gained 30 pounds and became diabetic. He quickly realized that fat wasn't the enemy, and this eventually led him to the research on wheat, which became the basis of *Wheat Belly*, which links blood-sugar-spiking wheat to his ill health. The fat that has been demonized over the past 40 years isn't associated with cholesterol and heart disease—it all goes back to the inflammation caused by unstable blood sugar levels. As I mentioned in the last section, low-fat diets are often not very satisfying. But if you add healthy fats to your diet, you not only feel satisfied but you support the health of your brain and nervous system.

Friendly Fats

Incorporating more healthy fats into your diet will give you the necessary ingredients to maintain a happy mood and good brain health. Here are some of my favorite healthy fats:

- Avocado and avocado oil

- Coconut oil

- Flaxseed oil

- Grass-fed butter

- Mayonnaise made with avocado oil

- Organic extra virgin olive oil

- Organic nut butters of all kinds

The one type of fat you absolutely must avoid is partially hydrogenated fat, like the kind found in many packaged baked goods and in margarine. This fat is not found anywhere in nature. It is a fake fat that doesn't get rancid. It is used in many prepackaged products because it extends shelf life. But do you really want to eat a product that doesn't expire until after you likely will?

Another thing to keep in mind is that when you eat fat, you shouldn't combine it with refined carbohydrates. Which means cheese is fine. Skip the crackers. Fruit and cheese, or vegetables and cheese are a much better option. Or make sure the crackers are made from legumes or seeds. The very worst foods for humans are the ones that are the most addictive—and the most widely available: sugar and fat combined. This includes donuts, pastries, and almost all baked goods. It also includes ice cream. This is where you remember the 80–20 rule. I intend to have a couple of ice-cream cones every summer. And a few baked goods as well. Especially brownies. And I bless them with Divine Love.

Rule 6: Cultivate the Right Germs to Ward Off the Bad

This is a big one: It is crucial that each of us learn how best to tend and feed our inner garden—our microbiome—the trillions of cells that line our guts and live in the openings of our bodies to protect us. When our microbiome is robust and healthy, it naturally keeps germs from becoming dangerous. In fact, healthy bacteria in our bodies—including healthy probiotic bacteria in fermented foods and in a healthy gut—actually contain what are called bacteriocins, good bacteria that attack pathogenic bacteria and keep everything under control. A healthy microbiome is the very best protection against disease. The health of our microbiome is so crucial to brain health that David Perlmutter, author of *Brain Maker*, has founded an entirely new medical society to study it.

We are at a crucial moment in human history as we emerge from the antibiotic era, realizing that the "war on germs" has had some dire and unintended consequences.

First and foremost is the fact that massive quantities of antibiotics are fed to livestock all over the world to make them grow bigger, faster. In fact, the majority of all antibiotics produced are for livestock. Plus, too many doctors—often caving to the demands of their misinformed patients—still prescribe antibiotics for conditions like the common cold, simply because patients have come to expect the antibiotic prescription. The end result is that we now have a global problem with superbugs—bacteria in our food supply and our bodies that are resistant to every known antibiotic out there, including the truly potent "last resort" ones. Pretty soon, the post–World War II miracle that saved so many lives and ushered in the era of modern medicine will have to undergo some radical changes.

So how do we counteract this war on bacteria? We need to eat foods that are loaded with probiotics—bacteria that contribute to a healthy gut, as well as a healthy genital, urinary, and respiratory tract. Make healthy fermented foods (which contain probiotics) a regular part of your diet. Commercial yogurt often has way too much added sugar. So stick with plain yogurt and sweeten it with stevia and berries. Kefir is also good, as are sauerkraut, kombucha, and kimchi. The canned varieties don't contain what you need. Choose products that are in the refrigerated aisle of the grocery store or make your own. There are so many good books and websites available about how to make fermented foods that you shouldn't have a problem finding them. In addition, you might want to add a good probiotic to your daily regimen to keep your microbiome in good shape. I especially recommend additional probiotics when traveling, because the stress of travel tends to kill off healthy bacteria.

Choosing a Good Probiotic

Here are a couple of things to keep in mind when searching for a probiotic to help balance your microbiome and amp up the numbers of good bacteria in your body.

- **Diversity of Strains:** A good probiotic should contain at least two different strains of healthy bacteria such as lactobacillus and bifidobacterium (e.g., B lactis, B bifidum, B longum). A combination of these two strains will support both the upper and lower gastrointestinal tract.

- **Potency:** Probiotic potency is measured in CFUs (colony-forming units). This figure should be listed on the label. Five billion CFUs is the low end for a daily maintenance dose. I'd suggest looking for something more in the range of 12 billion to 50 billion CFUs. And make sure this potency is guaranteed until time of expiration.

In addition to eating fermented food and taking a probiotic, you can add to your healthy bacteria by turning to Mother Earth herself. Eat produce right off the tree or out of the ground. Anthony William points out that there are millions of healthy bacteria on produce right as they are harvested. If you pick it and eat it from those sources whenever you can, you'll be seeding your ileum, a specific part of the small intestine, with healthy bacteria that go a long way to protecting your health.

Rule 8: Supplement Your Diet with the Right Stuff

In addition to probiotics, I take a number of other supplements, and I have for decades. There is absolutely no way that one can get optimal nutrition from food alone. Even when you eat organic most of the time, soils in which foods are grown have been depleted, so it's not as nutrition-packed as it used to be. Also, food loses nutrients when it's shipped or stored. You would have to eat enormous amounts of food to get anything close to optimal nutrient levels.

So here are the nutrient supplements I believe everyone needs:

- **A good multivitamin/mineral:** Look for supplements that are NSF GMP registered and pharmaceutical grade with guaranteed potency on the label. Evaluate your supplement based on the CAPPS formula: Completeness, Absorbability, Potency, Purity, Safety. I personally use USANA products and have for years. I have toured the facility in which they are produced and know all the nutritional scientists who make them. I like them so much that I'm actually an independent USANA distributor now. But USANA isn't the only good brand out there. I also like Metagenics. If you can't get these or if you're already using something and want to find out how good it is, consult the *Comparative Guide to Nutritional Supplements* by Lyle MacWilliam.

- **Iodine:** We need around 12.5 milligrams per day. If you have thyroid problems, start very slowly. Maine Coast dulse seaweed is a great source. I also use a type of liquid iodine called Survival Shield. One to two dropperfuls a day (available online).

- **Vitamin C:** Try to get 1,000–5,000 milligrams per day. I keep a large bottle of 1,000-milligram capsules of pure ascorbic acid at my house at all times. The brand I use is Pure Encapsulations. This vitamin is an über-antioxidant that is so potent at stopping infection that it was used decades ago intravenously to cure polio.

  When I feel a cold coming on—or feel run down in any way—I literally grab a handful of these vitamin C capsules. Sometimes I take up to 50 a day. You know you've reached tissue saturation when you get loose stools. Bowel tolerance varies among different individuals. Some can't tolerate more than 2,000 milligrams per day. But here's what you need to know: One mosquito bite will cause your serum vitamin C to plummet. So will one cigarette—or even secondhand smoke. So vitamin C is a kind of all-purpose natural preventive medicine cabinet!

- **Vitamin D:** We need 5,000 IU (international units) per day to maintain an optimal blood level of 40 to 85 ng/mL (nanograms per milliliter). It sometimes takes far more than 5,000 IU per day to get your blood levels optimal. Test kits for home testing are available at www.grassrootshealth.net, a site that houses the most cutting-edge vitamin D research in the world. Note: Optimal levels of vitamin D decrease your risk of cancer, heart disease, and multiple sclerosis (MS) by 50 percent! Regular sun exposure—working up to 20 to 30 minutes, three times per week, over as much of your body as possible during the summer months, also greatly reduces your risk for cancer and other health problems. Thirty minutes of sun exposure will give you about 10,000 IU of vitamin D production underneath your skin. Avoid sunburn; research now shows that the increased risk of skin cancer from sun exposure is greatly outweighed by the other health benefits of sunlight. And the adverse effects of avoiding the sun are so robust that lack of sunlight has been compared to smoking as a risk factor for diseases ranging from cancer to tuberculosis.

- **Magnesium:** Most people are deficient in magnesium, which is essential for many different enzymatic reactions in the body and for providing energy to your cells. Magnesium is also necessary for optimal nerve conduction. You can take magnesium in pill form—1,000 to 2,000 milligrams per day. Magnesium glycinate pills are very absorbable. You can also ingest this supplement in a drink. There are little packets of magnesium, called CALM, which you can put in water to drink. Quite delicious.

There are many others, of course, but this is a good baseline.

Bathe for Your Health

You can up your magnesium intake and relax your body and mind all at the same time with an Epsom salt bath. Epsom salt is actually magnesium sulfate, and it can be used as a magnesium supplement. Simply dissolve one to two cups of Epsom salt in a nice warm bath, and then soak for 20 luxurious minutes, which is ample time for the magnesium to be absorbed through your skin.

The Joys of Food and Eating

While the rules we've just talked about cover the "what" of eating—what you should put in your body so it has the building materials it needs—there is also some magic in the "how" of eating.

The age-old custom of breaking bread together—even if you skip the bread—aids digestion and adds ceremony, pleasure, connection, and love to a meal. What sounds better? Downing your perfect green juice as you dash for the subway or sitting down and calmly enjoying a cup of tea and a healthy meal with good friends? Studies have shown that when you eat with others, even if they are strangers, your digestion improves. Dr. Mario Martinez points out that rituals of pleasure—enjoyed every day—are a key component of the lifestyles of healthy centenarians, some of whom also enjoy a daily cigar or a glass of whiskey.

If you associate eating with pleasure and health rather than guilt and frustration, you can experience the true joys of eating. Countries like Spain, France, and Italy are masters at this. And when pleasure is your focus, you can be happy with yourself as you are now. Fulfillment in life should not be based on your size—even though many people live this way.

My daughter and her husband both went on a rigorous diet and weight-training program starting six months before their wedding. They looked spectacular. Both had six-pack abs and better bodies than they had ever had. So what did my daughter learn? That she can have a bikini body that looks like it's out of a magazine. What else did she learn? Keeping that body was a full-time job. It was a career. It meant weighing and measuring all her food and spending hours per day in the gym. And never just ordering what she wanted at a restaurant. It wasn't worth it, and it didn't make her happy. She now has a new baby, and a new life. And her body looks fantastic. It's not the magazine-perfect body she had before, but she doesn't care. She's happy and healthy.

The concept of "ideal weight" is kind of like the research on happiness. Everyone thinks they'll be happy when they get the right job, the right mate, and the right house. But the truth is that *happy* has to come first. Then and only then will you be in a position to attract the right mate or eat the foods that truly sustain you while maintaining optimal health. In other words, you have to figure out what's "eating you." When you attend to what's eating you, you'll finally know how to feed your body. And if you stick with whole foods most of the time, you'll be fine.

I'm healthy, a normal size, and I no longer weigh myself.

CHAPTER 11

Tending Your Vital Life Force

So really it happens that the more sexual a person is, the more inventive he can be. The more sexual a person is, the more intelligent. With less sex energy, less intelligence exists; with more sexual energy, more intelligence, because sex is a deep search to uncover, not only bodies, not only the opposite sex body, but everything that is hidden.

— Osho

Our vital life force—sometimes known by the Sanskrit word *shakti*—is the creative surge that comes through our bodies, minds, and Spirits as physical pleasure, desire, excitement, sexuality, and curiosity. It manifests as music, design, relationships, architecture, books, inventions, scientific breakthroughs, and creative endeavors of all kinds. On a purely physical level, it is the force that leads to the reproduction of the species.

But our vital-life force is far more than that. As the direct felt connection between our Spirits and our bodies, this force is the desire to express all of who we are—physically, mentally, and spiritually. Our vital life force fuels our bodies and keeps us engaged in living fully. When we are in touch with this force, we experience life as a grand adventure that is worth living. It is the elusive "will to live" that so often defies a doctor's dire prognosis and results in individuals living years longer than predicted. Stephen Hawking, the renowned physicist, is a great example. When he was first diagnosed with amyotrophic lateral sclerosis (ALS) decades ago, he was given two to three years to live. ALS has no known cause and no known cure in standard medical thinking, yet Hawking has gone on to have four children, two marriages, and a brilliant career. This was in part because he maintained a strong connection with his life force and sexuality.

Our creative fire needs to be tended, contained, cultivated, and consciously directed on a regular basis. When that flame is burning brightly, when we have a robust will to live or a purpose that drives us onward with curiosity and passion, then it almost doesn't matter what our physical bodies are like. On the other hand, when that flame dies, no vitamins, exercise, or desire from others will stop someone from dying—even if they remain in their bodies for years.

Your vital life force is the fire within. How comforting that fire is when harnessed consciously. It keeps you warm. It fuels good digestion (known as digestive fire). It feels good both in and outside of your body. It creates bonds of pleasure that enhance relationships. Basically, it makes life worth living on all levels. Think about how you feel when you first meet that new special someone. In the throes of a new relationship, the stars are brighter, you feel so full you don't need to eat, and all the love songs in the world feel as though they've been written for you. That's what life is like when you skillfully use your vital life force.

The Sex Drive: Why It's So Compelling

You've heard the expression "sex sells," right? Here's why: On a primal level, we understand that sex is associated with our vital life force. Our physical bodies were conceived through sex, and in representations of sex—wherever they appear—we recognize the force that ushered us into physical form. Sexual expression and the feelings associated with it—being hot and turned on—are simply the physical indicators of vital life force. When we see a sexy advertisement or an erotic movie, or when we read an erotic book, the messages within remind us of our inherent creative power and how delicious it is to connect with that feeling of pure aliveness and ecstasy.

When we start to feel the power of our vital life force in our attraction to someone else, our sex drive is so powerful that we will do whatever it takes to be with that person and express our desire physically. Even if we're working full time, have family responsibilities, and barely have enough time to sleep, we'll figure out a way.

Sexual attraction—and that "can't eat, can't sleep" high that you feel—is associated with a powerful brain chemical known as DMT (dimethyltryptamine). DMT is produced in the pineal gland, which is known in esoteric circles as the third eye, or sometimes the Eye of Horus. This gland begins to form in the brain when the fetus is 49 days old, which is also the time when the Tibetan Buddhists say the Soul enters the body. Talk about a powerful symbol. And it's only appropriate for the source of such a powerful hormone.

Interestingly, DMT is the most potent psychedelic substance known to man. It has been found to not only stretch time but also bring to life the deeply held religious beliefs of the people who smoke it. If they believe in angels, they see angels. Same with Jesus or Buddha. When DMT is synthesized in a lab, it is listed as a Schedule 1 addictive drug. But in humans, it's naturally produced in people who are in love. It's also produced in massive quantities during orgasm. And, believe it or not, at the moment we die. After this moment there are a few minutes where the brain hasn't shut down fully, and during this time, DMT courses through the brain, bringing with it the visions of your core beliefs that seem to last forever, thus our supposed move into heaven or hell. It is funny that the French call orgasm *la petite mort*—"the little death." Just like those last minutes after death, in orgasm we lose ourselves— for a time—and are freed from the cage of our egos so that we can experience the bliss consciousness we were born with.

The association of DMT with sex explains why sex—and various types of pornography—can become addictive, especially when they're used to avoid the Soul work for which we took birth.

Sexuality and Spirituality

The deep connection between sexuality and spirituality doesn't lie merely in DMT-induced religious visions. In fact, this association has been around for millennia.

In wisdom texts from India, Egypt, and other places, we see that puberty—when sexual desire begins to awaken strongly—is when the spiritual energy known as kundalini energy starts to rise up through the body. The texts depict this energy as a snake curled up at the base of the spine. Throughout puberty this snake rises through the spine, enlivening each area—and chakra—that it reaches. When kundalini energy is flowing freely through all of the chakras, it reaches the crown chakra and an individual is considered enlightened.

In a more modern look at the connection, we can turn to the landmark study entitled "Integrating Sexuality and Spirituality," which was led by Harvard researcher Gina Ogden. In this study, which was one of the largest ever done on this topic, they found that both men and women experience their sexuality as a deeply spiritual experience that connects them to God.

In her book *Angel Blessings*, Kimberly Marooney explains the roles of each of the many angels assisting us here on earth and the imagery and terminology she uses are the same as that you would use for sex. For example, she describes how the angel known as Nathaniel and his Amfri angels help you prepare your consciousness by burning up your self-imposed beliefs and limitations so that you are ready for the intensity of this vital life-force fire to enliven you. Marooney writes, "During this baptism, you may feel overwhelmed by the rapture of unconditional love. Let it erupt into a wild dance of passion and ecstasy that explodes in pleasure with the magnitude of its intensity. So much gratitude will pour into your heart that your chest will heave in orgasm and you will feel as if your body is merely a tube through which this energy travels."

Sounds exciting, doesn't it?

Sublimating the Sex Drive

While it might be easy to lose yourself in orgasmic bliss, this isn't a healthy way to live. The beauty of the sex drive is that it needn't result in sex. You can transmute it when necessary, routing the energy it provides into creative endeavors that bear fruit other than babies or orgasms. In the classic *Think and Grow Rich* by Napoleon Hill, there is a chapter entitled "The Mystery of Sex Transmutation (The Tenth Step to Riches)." The chapter begins by explaining the meaning of the word *transmutation*. Transmutation is the change or transferring of one element or form of energy into another. Hill writes:

> The emotion of sex brings into being a state of mind. Because of ignorance on the subject, this state of mind is generally associated with the physical, and because of improper influences, to which most people have been subjected, in acquiring knowledge of sex, things essentially physical have highly biased the mind.

Hill then explains that there are three constructive uses for sex: (1) The perpetuation of the human species, (2) the maintenance of sound physical and emotional health, and finally (3) the transformation of mediocrity into genius through transmutation.

By transmutation, Hill is not speaking of celibacy or the repression of natural instincts. Instead, transmutation is the ability to channel sexual energy and sexual desire into keen imagination, courage, willpower, and creative ability. This requires the will to harness and redirect sexual desire into a profession or a calling . . . including the creation of wealth.

Interestingly, when the sex drive is new—and the kundalini life-force energy of youth is on the rise—the transmutation of sexual energy becomes the focus of the world in which teens live. Most cultures have created structures designed to help channel this force constructively—or at least make teens too tired to do anything with it. Of course for most of human history, people married soon after puberty, so societies didn't have years and years where they were expected to sublimate their sex drives. Today, sports, dancing, and after-school activities of any kind aim to give young people other, more constructive, outlets for using their sexual energy. The expectation is that with all the practices and workouts and obligations required, kids would barely have time to do their homework, much less have sex with each other. Of course it's not a perfect world, so sometimes this doesn't work either.

While this structure may prevent a lot of unplanned pregnancies or other regrettable mishaps of youth, it does nothing to teach people the power of their sex drive in its own right, or as an influence for other creative pursuits. Kids would be better served by a vision quest or coming-of-age ceremony that would serve as a container to channel their vital life force in a meaningful way. This would help usher them into the offices of manhood or womanhood in a way that is uplifting, healthy, and empowering.

To fully feel at home with the power of our vital life force, and its manifestation as sexual energy, we need to acknowledge that adolescence is more than a hormone-fueled time of chaos. It is when a huge download of spiritual-sexual energy is entering the body. To use this energy wisely, kids need guidance and some really solid information. Being told "Don't come home pregnant" just doesn't cut it. While a few models do exist, including the Navajo Kinaalda coming-of-age ceremony for girls and the Jewish bat mitzvahs and bar mitzvahs, overall our culture hasn't done a very good job of honoring the creative sexual and spiritual fires of young men and women (or older ones, for that matter). The teaching we provide around sexual energy centers on shame, doubt, and embarrassment—not to mention the sexual abuse and incest that is too often handed down in families in desperate need of sexual healing. Because of all these things, most people don't have the ability to transmute sexual energy very well. There is so much fear, judgment, shame, and misunderstanding about sexuality and spirituality that it clogs the channels of the body. And these misunderstandings are passed down from generation to generation in families, religion, and culture.

Blockages of Vital Life Force

Situations where people aren't able to healthfully transmute their sexual energy, to skillfully contain and direct their vital life force, can end pretty dramatically. Remember that vital life force is fiery, so it can metaphorically burn down your house. For example, if your husband has sex with your best friend, then the fire of that passion, and the secrets, anger, and hurt that may result, can wreck both your friendship and your marriage—and adversely affect your children for generations to come, depending on how the situation is handled.

Pretty much everyone I know has been singed by the flames of a vital life force that wasn't used or handled wisely. Whether from well-intentioned protective shaming during adolescence or from something as terrible as rape or molestation, trauma to our vital life force manifests in the body. Chances are pretty good that you have some blockages in the areas of your body that are associated with your vital regenerative life force—your genitals, anus, and buttocks. Pretty much everything below the waist. And for women, your breasts as well.

We see these blockages in things like numb vaginas, poor pelvic muscle tone, and chronic pelvic pain. These are problems that so many women face. Women who have been sexually abused tend to store their pain—emotional and physical—in the fascia in the pelvis. And in the G-spot in particular.

In men, I have seen a lot of problems come from the trauma of circumcision, which is completely unnecessary medically. This procedure was popularized in the United States by the same Kellogg who invented Kellogg's Corn Flakes, and the main reason for it was to stop masturbation. In girls, he recommended pouring carbolic acid over the genitals. The reason circumcision caught on is because of the sexual shame that runs through our culture. And it has persisted because of a great deal of misinformation.

The numbers of infant boys having the procedure has steadily dropped—even among Jews. But still a huge number of men have had the erotic area of the body known as the prepuce removed without anesthesia. And this has emotional and physical consequences.

First and foremost, it is incredibly painful and it is done without the consent of the individual. Every time I've talked with a circumcised man about this, he looks down and often makes some kind of unconscious gesture—like tapping his feet or tapping his fingers on a table. Our bodies remember everything. And having this done to you is a setup for resentment and anger, especially against women.

In the physical realm, circumcision removes a very significant amount of erotic protective tissue. The result is that the head of the penis becomes hardened and numb compared to how it would be with an intact foreskin. When an intact man has intercourse with a woman, the foreskin clings to the rugae (folds) of the vagina in a way that provides more stimulation and intimacy.

I regret that I performed so many circumcisions as part of my career, and I truly apologize to all the men who underwent this procedure—both under my care and that of my colleagues.

Whether or not you've been outright sexually abused, chances are good that you've been subjected to shame somewhere along the line. And this lives in the body and blocks free-flowing vital life force. My first book, *Women's Bodies, Women's Wisdom*, was inspired by the connection between these traumas and our health. It astounded me that almost no one was talking about how the common gynecological disorders suffered by so many women were directly related to their experiences as women in a patriarchal culture.

The Healing of Pleasure

The blockages we experience in our vital life force make it hard for so many people to experience the fullness of life. They feel depressed, empty, or simply in a rut, and they also have trouble accessing their erotic potential. But experiencing the pleasure of our vital life force is important and extremely healing. When I say that pleasure heals, it's not just wishful thinking.

When I first began teaching at Mama Gena's School of Womanly Arts, a school that teaches women how to use pleasure as power, I knew nothing about the healing potential of pleasure and the vital life force associated with it. But as I watched the radiance of the participants, it dawned on me that what they were doing at the school was most likely having a physical healing effect. And so, during my lecture, I asked the women if any of them had experienced a significant healing since starting at the school. A line formed at the microphone that went to the back of the room. Women recounted how the deliberate pursuit of pleasure and the connection with their erotic life force had assisted in healing everything from lung cancer, bowel cancer, and abnormal Pap smears, to infertility. That got my attention, big-time.

Because I like to understand just why these things happen, I did some research, and I subsequently learned that the mechanism for this is nitric oxide. Nitric oxide is a gas produced in the lining of the blood vessels during pleasurable or healthful activities like exercise, sex, meditation, and sustainable pleasure of all kinds. Its production results in enhanced blood flow throughout the body. And also, since nitric oxide is an über-neurotransmitter, it balances serotonin, dopamine, endorphins, and the other feel-good chemicals made in both the brain and body. Nitric oxide is the molecule of life force. It is produced in large amounts during orgasm and also when the egg and the sperm connect. And like DMT, it is also present in large amounts at the moment of death. The body is a pretty spectacular thing.

It's amazing to see the power of pleasure firsthand. When a woman initially allows herself to bring consciousness and pleasure into the areas of her body that have brought her so much pain and shame, she will very often find herself sobbing with release. It has been said that the blood of the wound contains the healing. To me that means having the courage to bring healing pleasure into an area of the body that has been shut down with pain and shame.

For men who are in relationship with women who've been sexually abused, it's important to know that their attention and love can bring enormous healing for their partners. In fact, the penis is sometimes known as the "wand of light." In a loving relationship, that organ can be profoundly and deeply healing to a woman. I even had one woman tell me that when her husband massages her forehead with his erect penis, her headaches go away. Talk about sexual healing!

Luckily getting in touch with your vital life force through pleasure is something that everyone—of every gender and every age—can do anytime.

Connecting with Your Vital Life Force

To connect with your vital life force there are four keys: (1) turning yourself on to life, (2) deliberately pursuing pleasure, (3) engaging in mindful sexual expression, and (4) learning how to own and operate your erotic anatomy. Let's take these one at a time.

Key #1: Turn Yourself On to Life

Your vital life force—your "turn-on"—is an expression that is unique to you regardless of your gender, sexual orientation, or anything else.

So begin to notice what turns you on. What makes you feel most alive? That feeling is your vital life force in full effect. If you begin to notice when this happens, you can use it to guide your life. If something makes you feel more alive, go toward that. If it feels deadening, do less of it and leave it behind. Lying in the sun at the beach might be your thing, working in a greenhouse and smelling the rich soil, browsing in a bookstore, getting a massage or a foot rub, going to a dance class, listening to music and dancing.

Interestingly, women can use their bodies as a barometer to help them figure out what turns them on. When a woman experiences something pleasing, she can actually experience a distinctive pulse in her vagina. This is what sex researchers call the VPA (vaginal pulse amplitude). These researchers have documented measurements for the VPA with a device, known as a vaginal photoplethysmograph, that measures blood flow in the vagina. What I find most fascinating about this pulse, which Naomi Wolf calls the brain-vagina connection in her book *Vagina*, is that once women know about it, they don't have any trouble feeling it—and noting when they feel the pulse most strongly. Wolf's research found that women feel it most strongly when they are in situations in which they are emotionally safe and feel valued sexually. Examples include, "I felt it when my husband pulled out my chair" or "It was strong when my boyfriend threw a heavy couch out of the back of the truck." In other words, we feel that pulse—that turn-on—when we're with someone who is demonstrating his (or her) ability to care for us whether through strength or tenderness.

But we also feel it in entirely nonsexual ways. And this is key. The vaginal pulse can be felt when we encounter aesthetic beauty such as a sunrise or a beautiful painting. Or when listening to ecstatic music. A woman's relationship to her mind and body are erotic—long before there is any sexual connection with someone else. Our vaginal pulse is our inner barometer and indicator of our life force. It is a felt sense that not only lets us know how safe and valued we are but also connects us to the beauty and joy of living in a body. We can trust this pulse—this life force. You will find that it brings you a great deal of pleasure and delight.

To help you tune in to your turn-ons, for both men and women, put your focus on your genitals when you notice any feelings of vital life force in action—when you feel alive and vibrant. Energy flows where attention goes. Feel that generative area of your body. You'll probably feel a tingling sensation. Women may notice that pulsing VPA. Men may feel the beginning of an erection. After bringing your attention to your genitals, move that focus up to your heart. Go back and forth between those two places. Make this low heart-high heart connection. By doing this, you will expand your physical capacity to feel turned on—not just by physical sex—but by daily life. You will learn to make love to life itself.

Key #2: Pursue Pleasure Deliberately

Deliberately pursuing pleasure is something we often overlook in life, but it's essential if you want your vital life force to fuel you for a lifetime. So search out thoughts, relationships, and experiences that are pleasurable. This doesn't have to cost you a penny. You just need to set up your day so that you have experiences that bring you pleasure. That could mean you stand for 10 minutes on the grass and really feel how good that feels. Or you watch the sunset regularly. Or maybe you read a good book. Yes—a well-turned phrase is one of life's pleasures.

The important thing is that you don't wait until you're "on vacation" to indulge in pleasure. Make it part of your lifestyle. Simply focus on what feels or looks good; it doesn't take much time. Just focus.

When we think of pleasure, the first thing we often think of is sex. And though sex is right up there as very pleasurable, you'll find that your entire life—as well as your sex life—is enhanced by putting your attention on other things that are pleasurable besides sex. This practice of accessing all types of pleasure helps you be fully present when you are being sexual. And you'll find that you bring all those other pleasurable experiences to the bedroom.

I dance Argentine tango on a regular basis, and when I do I bring my full self to the dance, which makes it very pleasurable and sexy for me. During the dance, I am adding my life force—my shakti—to my partner, and my partner is adding his (or hers) to me. Occasionally there are couples who come to tango, and one or the other doesn't want their partner to dance with other people. They're too jealous. This is a profound waste of vital life-force. I always tell new couples that they should dance with lots of other people. Not only will it make them better dancers, it will also add immensely to their own personal relationship. They can take every drop of pleasure they felt on the dance floor back home to each other.

The number one so-called sexual dysfunction seen in women today is lack of desire. A new drug was just approved to treat it, but women don't need a drug. And quite frankly, most men don't need erectile-enhancing drugs either. What we all need is to be connected with our life force. We need to be present and alive in each situation. But you can't be present if you are spending all your time working, or worrying, or feeling resentful about everything you have to do. Changing your focus to pleasure and appreciation—starting with small things—can literally change your life.

Key #3: Engage in Mindful Sexual Expression

This is quite simple. When you are making love, including self-pleasuring, be present. Do no harm—to yourself or to another. Breathe deeply. And feel as much as possible.

The global popularity of the *Fifty Shades of Grey* trilogy speaks volumes about the different varieties of sexual expression that can be enjoyed. The books also say something important at the end of the story: No matter how many sex toys, positions, and devices you employ, love, caring, and genuine connection win. There is nothing more potent than the combination of love and sex—though they certainly can and do exist separately.

Part of mindful sexual experiences is making sure that you are happy and comfortable—and monogamy is actually an important part of this. My experiences with thousands of women (and some men) is that sexual expression tends to be safest and most creative when it has a solid container. That means one partner at a time—a monogamous pair bond. Though there are all kinds of ways to open up that container—sex parties, polyamorous communities, tantric workshops, and so on—the opening of the container on a regular basis is a lot like opening up the oven door repeatedly to see how the bread you're baking is coming along. The heat escapes and the quality of the bread suffers.

There are, of course, individuals who swear that they are very happy living in polyamorous communities in which everyone is having sex with everybody else. My experience with this is that the women involved are often trying to talk themselves into liking something that just doesn't feel right. But they want to be hip. And accepted. So they go along. But deep down, they're not happy about it. Yet they don't dare put their foot down lest they be rejected.

Therapist Pat Allen, author of *Getting to "I Do,"* takes this even further. She points out that a woman can essentially become addicted to the man she's having sex with. When a woman lets a man in sexually—as in intercourse—her brain produces large amounts of oxytocin, which has been linked with all forms of addiction. In addition, the cervix is the vaginal reflex area that corresponds to the heart, so when a man is inside a woman, he is literally stimulating her heart. This makes her more likely to fall in love with him.

This corresponds with the desire for monogamy that I've seen. Having a commitment is important to mindful sexual experiences. Allen teaches women who truly desire a solid committed relationship to avoid having intercourse with a man until he has made a commitment to her. The kind of man who is going to be capable of such a commitment is the kind who will cherish and protect her. He will only value a woman who values herself enough to require that commitment. One of the very hardest lessons for so many women is this one: We must value ourselves enough to be alone and hold out for a mate who truly cherishes us, versus staying in a bad relationship just to avoid being alone. To do this, you must learn to love, cherish, and value yourself first and foremost.

In my many years at the front lines of women's health, it has been my experience that the vast majority of women—and the men who love them—are looking for this kind of relationship, not a series of one-night stands or polyamorous orgies.

On another note, I'm also aware that there are all kinds of kinky practices that involve whips, chains, dominators, submissives, and everything else the human mind is capable of. And once again, what matters here is the solidity of the container in which these practices are carried out. In his illuminating book *Eleven Minutes*, the title of which refers to the average time the sex act takes, Paulo Coelho tells the story of a woman who was a sex worker in a brothel. When she was beginning this career she was cautioned not to go down the road of physical harm and degradation, even if it was requested by one of her clients. The reason was this: The darker you go, the darker it gets. And the abyss is endless. Enduring physical pain and shame so that another person can get sexually aroused creates great potential for harm. As with all addictions, more and more of the addictive substance or process is required over time in order to get the same effect. That said, if your container is stable, you can safely take part in watching porn or participating in sexual situations that involve pain, shame, and degradation. Just be selective if you choose to do this. And make sure that this choice is actually yours. And that your life is enhanced and uplifted as a result, not degraded.

A Word about Pornography

Pornography is as old as the human race. I was visiting the ancient city of Ephesus in Turkey a while back and the tour guide pointed out pornographic images painted on the walls of the bedrooms in an excavated home from the time of the Roman empire.

But the Internet has made it possible to view more sexually explicit images than ever before. The combination of repeated watching and an aroused state can rewire your brain and make you addicted to porn—the kind of porn in which the goal is getting a man's large penis in the vagina, mouth, or anus of a woman (or man) ASAP to reach the goal of his orgasm. Many young people's sexual education is now delivered through porn. And thus they do not acquire the skills, patience, caring, and attentiveness that produce orgasmic abundance and life-enhancing sex. Unfortunately, the more porn you see, the more you want to see to get the desired "hit"—especially if you are using pornography to avoid feeling deeply. So you have to be mindful about what you consume. And why. And remember not to judge your own sex life by what you see in these images. Don't allow yourself to get talked into something you don't want to do.

Truly erotic movies tend to focus on the tension and electromagnetic force that builds between people. I remember seeing the movie *Bright Star,* and when the poet John Keats first touched the hand of the woman who loved him, I literally felt a shock go through my body. I'd like to see more of this. Just beautiful. Life affirming. And intensely erotic.

Key #4: Owning and Operating Your Erotic Anatomy

So far, I've talked a lot about how to think about, sublimate, and channel your vital life force. Now I want to give you some hands-on instructions for what to actually do with your erotic anatomy physically that can help you light your fire in very pleasurable and healthful ways. Pleasure is a truly healing force, and it will often open up blocked areas of the body and the fascia in a way that nothing else can. I know it can be scary to fully access your sexual energy, but it's worth the effort to "go there." It will make you feel physically and emotionally more healthy and happy. Naomi Wolf has documented this beautifully in her classic book *Vagina.* Interestingly, enhancing your vital life force also tends to attract more money to you. You've heard the term "shake your moneymaker," right? If you want to make this literal, try self-pleasuring or making love on a pile of bills—I'm not kidding. This will solidify in your mind, this powerful connection. Watch what happens.

I recommend a regular practice of self-pleasuring in which you use your breath and sound to enhance pleasurable feelings. The idea here is to train your body to feel more and more—with less and less stimulation necessary. It is possible to have an orgasm simply from earlobe stimulation. Some people can even think themselves into an orgasm. We all have far more access to pleasure than we've been led to believe.

Aim for 30 minutes of practice two to four times per week. Start where you feel comfortable. You can always increase it. Your sexual relationship with yourself is different from any other sexual relationship in your life. If you have a sexual partner, they can join you—but the focus must be on your pleasure. If you do not have a partner, this practice will keep your juices flowing for a lifetime. And if and when a partner arrives, all of your equipment will be in top form.

Sex educator Sheri Winston points out that we can all learn to be sexual virtuosos. It just takes practice. Playing chopsticks on the piano is easy. But playing a concert at Carnegie Hall requires some focus and time. It's the same with having sex. Training your body to circulate sexual/erotic energy to use as vital fuel requires more than just "getting off." So here are some tips for successful self-pleasuring.

Microcosmic Orbit

Both men and women can benefit from doing the microcosmic orbit. This ancient practice is taught by practitioners of Taoist sexuality as a way to distribute sexual energy throughout your body. It's a simple exercise:

1. Put your tongue on the roof of your mouth, just in back of your front teeth. This completes the microcosmic orbit circuit that begins in your perineum and goes up your spine and down your front to your navel.

2. Contract your pubococcygeus (PC) muscle several times—this is the muscle that you use to stop the flow of urine. Do not tense your buttocks.

3. Now inhale your sexual energy up your spine—to the top of your head. Then down the front of your face to your navel.

4. Imagine a cauldron of sexual energy between your pubic bone and your navel. Imagine storing vital sexual energy there each time you do the exercise. You are building your vital life force this way, not depleting it.

5. Repeat this orbit several times.

You can also do the microcosmic orbit exercise during the day—especially when you are turned on. Use your imagination to move the energy.

I highly recommend the Universal Healing Tao System of Mantak Chia to learn more techniques like this one. You can learn more at www.multi-orgasmic.com.

Self-Pleasuring for Men and Women

Self-pleasuring is such an important part of owning and operating your erotic anatomy that I wanted to talk about it in quite a bit of detail. While many people refer to this process as masturbation, I like to avoid this word. Like the plague. I despise it because it is saturated with shame. *Masturbation* literally means "to defile with the hand." How can something so beautiful be referred to in this way? The ancient Taoists called self-pleasuring "self-cultivation," which I think is a much better term for what this experience can be about. Self-pleasuring is an essential part of both emotional and physical health, so let's get down to it.

For Men: While I don't feel like I need to address many of the specific mechanics of self-pleasuring for men—as most men are pretty skilled at this—there is one mechanical issue that I'd like to talk about. This is that the G-spot in men is in the anus. Some men avoid this when they are self-pleasuring because it's "weird," but the anus itself contains a lot of nerve endings. And the G-spot is just inside at about 12 o'clock. Stimulating the anus, especially the G-spot, can be very pleasurable. It's also good for prostate health. To successfully access the nerves in the anus, I recommend using one of two tools. One is the crystal wand and the other is the njoy.

Both can be found online. When you use them, make sure to use plenty of lube.

If you would like more information on self-pleasuring techniques for men, in the book *Orgasm Matters*, Steve Bodansky provides a wide range of them, including putting pressure on what he calls the "hidden cock," which is an internal extension of the penis right under the testicles on the perineum. Deep pressure there will massage the prostate. Pressing there will also help control ejaculation. Stimulation of this area with a lighter touch will allow you to experience more pleasure. Steve says it's pleasurable for most guys to pull on their testicles rather than push them into their body. Try it without lube and then with it to experience the difference.

Aside from the mechanics, men can benefit from learning how to maximize orgasm, and this can be done during self-pleasuring. Maximizing the length of time before an orgasm will intensify sexual sensation can work wonders to increase overall sexual energy. Relaxing and breathing fully are very important.

Drs. Steve and Vera Bodansky, authors of *The Illustrated Guide to Extended Massive Orgasm*, are pioneers in the study of orgasm and pleasure. They have taught hundreds of people to reach their orgasmic potential and heal their relationship to sexuality. They teach that most men experience orgasm like this: tense up and squirt. But this shuts down your capacity to feel and enjoy your vital life force. It needn't be this way.

There is an entire world of enhanced pleasure available to men who are willing to learn how to orgasm differently. In this instance, it's about having an orgasm without ejaculation. This will extend the length and sensation of pleasure available; it will also spread it throughout your body.

To do this, the key is to relax, breathe deeply, and really experience the place just before ejaculation. When you reach this place, contract your PC muscles multiple times—just like in the microcosmic orbit practice. This will make the sexual excitement wane a bit. Then you have the opportunity to build it up again. You can do this through the use of light strokes or more pressure, or by spiraling strokes down the entire length of the shaft. Bring the energy up and let it come down repeatedly before finishing off with ejaculation. Over time you will be able to prolong your erection for long periods of time—at will.

A man can also learn how to channel his sexual sensations throughout his entire body so that he feels pleasure in more areas. To do this, you bring yourself almost to orgasm—let's say an arousal state just before ejaculation but before you have gone over the edge where it's inevitable—perhaps a 7 on a scale of 1 to 10. Then you contract your PC muscle and stop stimulating yourself. Breathe fully while doing a couple of microcosmic orbits with your breath and imagination. Now start again. Doing this for several rounds will train your body to have greater control over ejaculation—and also will allow you to feel pleasure all over your body instead of just confining sensation to your genitals. Over time, with practice, you'll be able to train yourself to have an orgasm without ejaculating. This will render you able to make love for far longer.

In Mantak Chia's multiorgasmic man teachings, he suggests that men explore what he calls the "million-dollar point," which is just in front of the anus in the perineum. Pushing on this spot can help stop the ejaculatory reflex and squeeze more blood into the penis. The result is pleasurable throbbing that imitates the prostate contractions that accompany ejaculation. It's best to stimulate the million-dollar point after you have an erection and are highly aroused, because arousal and engorgement of tissue happens from the front of the body to the back.

Self-cultivation for men is described by many as somewhere between self-pleasuring and meditation. It is very different from the usual tension-relieving two- to three-minute quickies. It's very important to take as much time as you have to enjoy and learn how to prolong self-pleasuring. By doing this, you are circulating rejuvenating healing energy throughout your body.

You'll also be able to last longer during lovemaking. Chia reports that men who can prolong an erection and self-pleasuring for 15 to 20 minutes on their own can then go as long as they like during intercourse. The 15- to 20-minute time frame is key. And this takes pleasurable practice.

For men who are interested in learning more about prolonging orgasm, I highly recommend *The Multi-Orgasmic Man* by Mantak Chia and Douglas Abrams, *Orgasm Matters* by Steve Bodansky, and *Succulent SexCraft* by Sheri Winston and Carl Frankel.

For Women: The mechanics of self-pleasuring for women are less familiar because of the shame and judgment placed on women's sexual expression. In general, men self-pleasure far more frequently than women do, though there are certainly exceptions. Because of this, I want to walk through some specifics of how to create the most pleasurable self-pleasuring experience possible so you can get the full power of your vital life force on your side.

Set a Pleasurable and Beautiful Stage: I recommend that you create a place of restful beauty for your self-pleasuring. Use flowers, candles, incense, some lovely music—and a beverage of your choice. Make sure to have a good-quality oil or lotion available. I recommend pomegranate oil, but there are many other options. Google the topic and you will find a variety of products. Also have some lubricant, if desired. Clear the space of all clutter. Prepare it as though you were expecting a very important guest, because you are. You are that guest. Honor yourself in this way.

Start with Breast Massage: When you self-pleasure, start with breast massage. Use the oil or lotion you have and spend about five minutes on your breasts. You can simply do what feels good or you can use a structured method like the Female Deer Exercise outlined in the box on the following page. There are lots of great videos online that take you through various breast massage techniques—including the Female Deer Exercise.

Breast massage and nipple stimulation are very pleasurable for most women. Getting breast implants can decrease or eliminate nipple sensation quite dramatically—something to consider before having that procedure.

Female Deer Exercise

The Female Deer Exercise, which is an ancient Taoist practice, is very helpful for enhancing erotic energy. It is also beneficial for pelvic and breast health. Here's how it's done.

1. Sit in a cross-legged position on a pillow.

2. Put the heel of one foot against the opening of your vagina, pressing against the clitoris. Use a tennis ball if you can't get your heel in position.

3. With pressure against the clitoris, begin massaging your breasts in a circular motion. Start with your palms under your breasts, cupping them. Now move your hands out to the sides and come around the top and down again, completing the circle.

4. Do this mindfully and pleasurably 10 to 60 times. Then reverse directions. The nipples can be very sensitive, so avoid them for the moment.

5. Breathe fully and deeply.

You will find that this exercise is very arousing. You may find that you start to lubricate vaginally.

Move On to the Rest of Your Body: Now that you have massaged your breasts, chances are good that you're aroused. Now lie down and begin massaging your inner thighs, your abdomen, and all other areas that bring you pleasure. Do not touch your clitoral area just yet. Instead, play around with your pubic hair and other areas of your body. Keep breathing—slowly and deeply. If you feel like it, move your body sensually and languidly.

After about 10 to 15 minutes, find your clitoris—this is the only organ in the body with the sole function of pleasure. It has 8,000 nerve endings in it. You only see the tip of the clitoris on the outside of the body, but the clitoris is like an iceberg—most of it is deep inside where you can't see it. There is also erotic erectile tissue around the urethra and the anus. Women have as much erectile tissue as men, but it's all inside.

The clitoris comprises an entire system of erotic erectile tissue in the pelvis—extending out in two branches on either side, deep to the pubic bone and also to the urethra and anus. There are many branches of the pelvic nerve that innervate the different areas of the pelvis and erotic anatomy. The pelvic nerve arises from the lower spine and branches out in ways that are unique to each woman. Some have more nerve sensation around their clitoris, some their vaginas, some their G-spot. And some their perianal area. That's why it's so important to explore and get to know your own erotic anatomy.

There is a spot on the clitoris, just to the left of center, at about one o'clock (with the clock facing away from you), that is the most sensitive spot for most women. Slowly and gently begin massaging this area. Keep everything deeply relaxed. Do not tense your legs or your buttocks. Just keep breathing and enjoying the sensation. Do not try to have an orgasm but go ahead and enjoy one if you so desire. As you are self-pleasuring, practice the microcosmic orbit to move your sexual energy.

Your self-pleasuring can involve the G-spot if you'd like. In women, the G-spot can be felt when you are in an aroused state just behind the pubic bone. It's about the size of a quarter. If you squat down and put your fingers in your vagina, hooking them up under the pubic bone, you will feel the G-spot as a slightly raised, highly pleasurable area. Stimulation of the G-spot stimulates the pineal gland energetically, which in turn produces that wonderful chemical DMT. There is a tool called a crystal wand that you can get online to help you stimulate that area as part of your self-pleasuring. There is also one called njoy. Stimulation of the G-spot is what produces female ejaculation—I'm not talking orgasm here; that can be experienced by stimulation of other areas of the body too. Female ejaculation comes from G-spot stimulation. The ejaculate, which is produced in copious amounts, may feel like urine, but it's extremely different. In ancient texts it is called Amrita—and it was considered very beneficial to consume.

Keep stimulating your clitoris, G-spot, or other erotic anatomy in a pleasurable way to wake up your body. It's fine to have an orgasm, but it's not necessary. The entire point of this exercise is to get your shakti flowing and circulating throughout your body. It will also help train your body to receive more pleasure.

Note: When you first start stimulating your G-spot, you may notice that it is numb or even painful. That's because this is where women often store unresolved pain from past sexual experiences or shame. Don't let this deter you. Keep bringing love and attention to the area. It will wake up and you will discover bliss here. If you are in a relationship that is safe and committed, you might ask your partner to stimulate this area for you while you simply receive his or her touch and feel pleasure. Doing so—without the goal of intercourse—can work wonders for the health of a relationship.

The Benefits of Vaginal Penetration

If you are a woman and do not have a sexual partner, I recommend that you use a dildo from time to time while self-pleasuring. The silicon ones are the best in that they are easy to keep clean. You can use a dildo as part of your self-pleasuring practice. There are vaginal reflex zones that correspond to all your major organs—just like the reflexology points on your hands and feet. Keeping them stimulated when you have intercourse or use a dildo is good for your health since it tones all the organs of the body.

I do not, however, recommend the use of vibrators during your self-pleasuring sessions. Over time, vibrators can actually dull sensation, not enhance it. As that happens, you require more and more stimulation to feel less and less. The goal is to train your body to swoon at the slightest erotic touch. Or thought.

Maintaining Physical Health of Your Erotic Anatomy

The last bit of information I want to share about owning your erotic anatomy is solely for women. As I mentioned at the beginning of this chapter, many women I've worked with have numb vaginas and poor pelvic muscle tone. Luckily, this isn't a permanent condition. You can wake your vagina up and increase your muscle tone by using a small device called a yoni egg.

The yoni egg is an ancient form of female sexual fitness that originated as a secret practice with the royal families of ancient China. Yoni egg practice keeps the pelvic floor muscles in great shape. It also helps prevent urinary stress incontinence and uterine prolapse.

Yoni eggs, which can be made out of jade, rose quartz, obsidian, or any other stone, are small egg-shaped devices with holes drilled in them that are inserted into the vagina. The simplest way to use the egg is to thread a piece of silk thread or dental floss through the hole so that it's easy to remove. Stand up and walk around with the egg in place for anywhere from 15 minutes to an hour or so. If you can't keep the egg in while standing, then lie down and practice keeping the egg in while pulling gently on the string. Over time, you will be able to strengthen your muscles to keep the egg in place while standing up. You can build even more strength and vaginal dexterity by tying some kind of weight to the string like a small bag of stones. Then you insert the egg into your vagina and use your vaginal muscles to hold it in. Simply walk around with it in your vagina for an hour or so. The act of holding the egg in place with the weights provides a powerful biofeedback mechanism that automatically strengthens your pelvic floor and vaginal muscles.

There are many other ways to use a yoni egg, and complete instructions generally come with the egg itself. Yoni eggs are easily obtained online.

Sharing the Love

While self-pleasuring is important to recharge your vital life force, there is something to be said for a shared experience of love and sex. Giving pleasure to someone you love recharges both of you.

I've talked with many spouses and partners throughout my years as an ob/gyn physician—what I've found most endearing about almost all of them is how much they want to provide pleasure for their partners. They want to be generous lovers. They also reiterated what I just said: They get as much pleasure from pleasuring their partners as they do from their own orgasms.

One of the interesting things I've come to realize, both from my own life and the lives of my patients, is that the pleasure women seek is often not purely physical. Most women thrive on attention—and we need it daily, in big and small ways. When someone pays attention to our pleasure, including admiring our bodies, we melt with appreciation. Words that express this can be simple—a sexy text to say you're thinking about her or a quick note that says how you can't wait to be with her when you get home will work wonders for your vital life force. And hers. The famous novelist Isabel Allende once wrote that the G-spot of a woman is in her ears. Anyone who looks for it elsewhere is missing the mark. There is such truth in this.

The smartest thing a man can ever do is to learn to love a woman well—with both his words and his body. (This applies to all humans, of course, whether gay, straight, or transgendered. Please change the pronouns as you desire.) A woman will reward such a man as her hero in ways that elevate him far beyond what he would otherwise be. The reason for this is that women (or the more yin member of a couple) are the real center of power. That old saying "The hand that rocks the cradle rules the world" has a great deal of truth in it—even though women haven't always been running countries or making the laws. Emotionally, however, women have a huge amount of power over a man's happiness and thus his vital life force. It has been found that married men are, overall, happier and healthier than their single counterparts.

One more thing you should know about a shared experience of pleasure is that the physical expressions of vital life force—feeling hot and turned on—are contagious. It is a turned-on woman who turns on a man—and vice versa. Our bodies are amazingly tapped into energy.

At one point in my life, I decided to work one-on-one with the Bodanskys, the authors of *The Illustrated Guide to Extended Massive Orgasm*, to bring life back to my nether regions. Steve and Vera's energy as a couple and their obvious love for each other was an inspiration. Married for many years, their strong, committed container has allowed them to assist others in reaching their own erotic potential in a safe way with healthy boundaries. I was also struck by the fact that Vera is 20 years older than Steve. This truly helped reset my idea of what is possible in a committed relationship, realizing that age need not be a factor.

The first thing they did was ask me to give them my sexual history. With the following instructions: I had to turn them on as I shared it. Yikes. I knew there was no way I could fake this. I actually had to feel erotic in my body as I spoke, making the connection between my thoughts and my erotic anatomy. And then Steve told me something that I don't think many women know—because I sure didn't. A man's penis can sense when a woman is turned on. It's like a sensual barometer. It quite literally responds to vital life force by becoming erect. This works with women as well—remember the VPA we discussed earlier.

So as you seek to live fully tapped in to your vital life force, allow your body to be your sensual barometer. Allow life force to flow through you. Enjoy it. Revel in it. It's yours. Own and operate it to live fully and pleasurably as a force for prosperity, pleasure, and joy.

CHAPTER 12

The Power of Community

*Healing is impossible in loneliness; it is the opposite
of loneliness. Conviviality is healing. To be healed we must
come with all the other creatures to the feast of Creation.*

— WENDELL BERRY

I have often said that community equals immunity. And it's
true. All humans thrive on real connection, acceptance, and intimacy. Our bodies are profoundly affected by our interactions with
those closest to us—our tribes. We are herd creatures, and with
few exceptions, we do best, physically, emotionally, and spiritually, when we are part of a tribe that values us.

There are hundreds of studies that prove how crucial social
connection is to our health, but I have a couple of favorites that
show this just beautifully.

One study done at Carnegie Mellon University in Pittsburgh
is called "Social Integration and Health: The Case of the Common
Cold." This study proved how profoundly our social networks
affect our immunity and resilience. The methodology was this:
They brought in a group of volunteers and assessed their social
diversity—meaning the quality and quantity of their social connections. Examples of this include family, church groups, dance
groups, work groups, and so on. Then the volunteers had cold
virus (rhinovirus) drops put into their noses. The researchers then
weighed the tissues used by participants to blow their noses—as a

measure of how severe the colds were that they developed. Over the course of the study, they found that the people who were least likely to experience cold symptoms—despite being exposed—were the ones who had the most robust and diverse social connections. This is why when someone says to me, "Oh, I don't want to give you a hug because I'm coming down with a cold," I tell them that I'm not worried. And it's true. I never, ever worry about catching a cold from someone because I know that there are so many other factors involved in immunity besides mere exposure to germs. (And yes, there is no question that washing your hands regularly decreases your chances of spreading germs around a school or a hospital.)

Another study I love is the longest-running study ever done on what creates health and happiness: the Harvard Study of Adult Development. This ongoing study started in 1938 with 724 men from two groups—those from Harvard and those from less privileged backgrounds in Boston. About 60 of the men from the original group were still living as of 2014. The study, which is now following the children of these men, found that those with the most solid relationships—with friends, family, and community—are the happiest and healthiest. It was determined that it is not the number of friends that influences one's health and brain function, but instead the quality of these relationships.

So Much More Than Germs

As we've discussed throughout this book, health and disease are far more complicated than just being exposed to germs. After all, there are three times as many germs in and on our bodies as there are cells. This is the microbiome we discussed earlier. The key to health is living in harmony with the communities of people around us—and also with the communities of microorganisms within and around us. The harmony within these communities is far more important than the individual germs that grow there.

There's a famous argument that happened between two prominent scientists in the 1800s: Antoine Béchamp and Louis Pasteur.

Béchamp argued that it wasn't a specific germ that caused a disease. It was, instead, the environment in which that germ found itself. Pasteur argued that it was the germ. He was, after all, the guy who invented the process known as pasteurization. But on his deathbed Pasteur admitted that Béchamp had been correct all along. The environment is indeed more important than the germ itself. Most people have forgotten this truth in our era of über-sanitation, which involves spraying ourselves and all the surfaces around us with disinfectant. And being injected with an ever-increasing number of vaccinations—all driven by our cultural belief in our universal vulnerability to germs.

The truth is that we are all exposed to disease-causing germs each and every day. Whether or not we get sick has a whole lot to do with the quality of our community interactions, both inside and outside of our bodies.

In the end, love and connection win, which was proven, yet again, by another of my favorite studies on this topic. The Ohio State University rabbit study clearly showed the impact of human interaction on health—even though the original intent of the study was to study the disease process leading to cardiovascular disease. This study involved a group of rabbits, all of which were bred to be highly susceptible to heart disease and hardening of the arteries. Then they were fed various diets that would promote heart disease.

At the end of the study, the rabbits were all sacrificed so their arteries could be examined microscopically. All the rabbits should have shown signs of cardiovascular disease—and most of them did. But there was one group whose arteries were clean and unaffected. No one could figure out why. And so the study was repeated. And then repeated again with the same result. What was going on? It was soon discovered that the group of rabbits with clean arteries and no disease were the ones whose cages were easily accessible to a female graduate student who fed them every night. But she did more than that. She petted them and played with them. That social interaction is what kept them healthy—despite their genes and their poor diets. When presenting this data in lectures, I like to say, "So if you're going to have a meal that puts you at risk for heart disease, then be sure to schedule a massage."

The Cost of Not Having Community and Connection

Back when my daughters were in school, I told them that kids did drugs, smoked cigarettes, and used alcohol because, for the most part, they felt unhappy. They were using these substances as a way to deal with their pain. I also told them how peer pressure works. If you feel bad about yourself and want desperately to fit in, you'll be vulnerable to peer pressure to do all kinds of things that aren't sustainable or healthy. Why else would you try to prove how cool you are by using a substance that contains dozens of toxins, wrecks your lung capacity, and shuts down your heart? No healthy mammal would ever do this. I've even known dogs who won't touch some of the most popular fast foods because the dog's instincts tell them that that food isn't healthy.

Addictive substances like cigarettes, drugs, and alcohol are widely available everywhere. And what I've seen is that they become real problems when the people in the community lack solid connections.

In his illuminating TED talk called "Everything You Think You Know about Addiction Is Wrong," Johann Hari recounts his years studying the addiction research that has been used to justify the current treatment of addicts, which is mostly punitive. He points out that addictive drugs like cocaine and heroin don't cause addiction. If you've ever had surgery, chances are good that you've been given morphine or some derivative of heroin. When you have acute post-op pain, there is nothing better. But it won't cause addiction unless there is already an underlying problem.

Our current treatment models for addiction simply do not address the underlying problem—the feeling of alienation from our lives, our work, and the lives of others and the emotional pain that results from this. The brain registers emotional and physical pain in the same area, and emotional pain can be just as painful as physical pain. It is those with unremitting emotional pain who are at risk for addiction. When rats are isolated in cages and given a choice between water laced with heroin or plain water, they pick the drugged water every time. And they end up killing themselves. But when they are put in enriched environments with plenty of toys and social interaction, they ignore the drugged water. There are now better ways to enjoy themselves.

Addictions—whether to sugar or cocaine or work or sex—are associated with emotional pain and emptiness, which come through a lack of community connection and validation. And also ignorance of the vast resources and guidance each of us has within ourselves. The substance or process that an addict is hooked on is used as a solution to their pain—but is not the cause of it. Vincent Felitti, M.D., who initiated the huge Adverse Childhood Experiences (ACE) Study, has documented this beyond a shadow of a doubt. The more adverse childhood experiences someone has—e.g., divorce, watching a parent get beaten or yelled at, poverty, mental illness in the family, chronic illness, and so on—the more apt they are to become addicts, experience medical emergencies, get ill, and die prematurely.

Wendell Berry said it brilliantly in *The Art of the Commonplace*: "People use drugs, legal and illegal, because their lives are intolerably painful or dull. They hate their work and find no rest in their leisure. They are estranged from their families and their neighbors. It should tell us something that in healthy societies drug use is celebrative, convivial, and occasional, whereas among us it is lonely, shameful, and addictive. We need drugs, apparently, because we have lost each other."

Johann Hari tells us that a while back Portugal decided to decriminalize drugs and drug addicts, and instead of putting addicts in jail, they used the money they saved to help them reconnect with the community and become gainfully employed. The result has been a 50 percent reduction in the number of people using drugs. This is a beautiful example of how compassion, not shame, and love, not censure, actually heals the problem at its source. Not always, of course. But far more often than the old shaming model.

I've come to believe that pretty much everyone—at least in Western culture—is addicted to something at some point in their lives. The root cause of all these addictions was stated beautifully by a friend of mine who goes to Alcoholics Anonymous meetings. She said, "I seem to make everyone and everything my Higher Power except for my real Higher Power." That's why it has been said that "addiction is God's answer to community." At a 12-step meeting or support group, you can be vulnerable and honest. True connection and intimacy are the result.

Finding the Love

The late Elisabeth Kübler-Ross, who pioneered the study of death and dying, said that our society raises its children to be little prostitutes by using variations of "I'll love you if [blank]." This encourages us to think that we're flawed, that we can't trust ourselves, and that we must look for acceptance from outside of ourselves. We forget that we are enough just as we are, and overcoming this belief is a big reason why we were born in the first place. So there are no mistakes here. No blame, no shame when you look at this from your Soul's point of view. But we must remember that who we are is important, and unless we are part of a tribe that is aligned with our Soul, no amount of acceptance and approval will matter.

Let me give you an example. I got pneumonia about 10 years ago because I was determined not to endure tribal shaming by showing physical weakness and vulnerability. I got sick because I put community obligation ahead of my own physical well-being—something I had learned very well in medical school. Doctors aren't allowed to call in sick.

I had committed to meeting a group of businesspeople in New York City to discuss a potential deal. I was also scheduled to receive an award for being a pioneer in Functional Medicine. I had just returned from Denver several days before, where I had participated in a group in which I felt undervalued and exploited.

I came down with a cold while there. The hotel was also cold, and I couldn't seem to get warm.

When I arrived home, I got right into bed, knowing that my recovery depended on resting for at least 24 hours. I was scheduled to go to New York three days later. If things had worked out as planned, I would have recovered, but a snowstorm was coming. I knew that if I didn't get to New York a day early, all the flights would be canceled on the scheduled departure date.

So I arose from my bed—dizzy and aching—and flew to New York. Then I bulled my way through my obligations—coughing and nearly unable to speak. And slogging through snow and wind that made it impossible to find a cab.

After finally getting home, I collapsed in bed with pneumonia. Something I thought I could beat if I just kept trucking, but it ended up beating me. My lungs didn't heal fully for a year, and they've been vulnerable ever since. Had I listened to my body and cared for myself when I needed to, rather than give in to my perceived tribal obligations, I never would have developed pneumonia. But in my personal tribe at that time, people who canceled things because of illness were considered weak and unworthy. I remember once seeing a T-shirt on a Marine that read "Pain is weakness leaving the body."

The belief system of my tribe back then—fully supported by me—was that caring for my body and my health through rest and sleep was not a worthy goal. It was a sure sign of weakness and laziness. You pretty much had to be on your deathbed to warrant the luxury of rest. One of my father's favorite sayings when I was growing up was "Don't ask for a lighter pack. Ask for a stronger back." There's wisdom in there, of course. But not in every situation.

Simone Weil put the human tendency to try to fit in quite hauntingly: "The danger is not lest the soul should doubt whether there is any bread, but lest, by a lie, it should persuade itself that it is not hungry." We are all hungry for genuine connection and caring, and we will not get this unless we find our Soul's tribe. If we don't find this, we'll kill ourselves, either by finding an addiction to mask the pain or by ignoring what we need to stay healthy.

The New Tribe Emerges

We are now at a critical turning point in history. People are waking up all over the planet. Spiritual groups of all kinds are forming in which people get together to honor themselves and the planet. The age-old form of tribalism in which we separate ourselves into small groups that war against one another and also sacrifice our own innermost desires in order to fit in is now giving way to a different kind of tribalism. A tribalism in which more and more of us realize that we are all part of humankind and that Mother Earth is our support system. We're part of her and she is part of us. Our earth is not divided into different tribes. We are all one. Just as rivers aren't divided into different countries. Mountain ranges run through many different territories and countries. What unites us is far more powerful than what separates us. Despite what the mainstream media would have you believe.

The astounding research of people such as Larry Dossey, the author of *One Mind*, has documented that on some fundamental level we all share the same mind, and what happens to one of us affects us all.

Many people have grown up in families and tribes that separate them from others, not unite them. They've been taught that their God is the right God. That their way of life is the right one; everyone else is wrong. Or they've been taught that the Creator is a mean, judgmental force that will inevitably find them unworthy. Luckily the old zero-sum model (there's only so much to go around, so we better grab ours while we can) is giving way to a different way of thinking. We are beginning to see that there is indeed enough to go around. It is not about "the person who dies with the most toys wins." New ways of marketing goods and services are arising in which everyone prospers, instead of a few people at the top making all the money. Network marketing and affiliate marketing are great examples. These models work through cooperation, not competition. They also provide work environments marked by friendship and intimacy.

Finding Your True Tribe

During this transition period from the old tribalism to the new, it's extraordinarily important to understand the limits of your cultural programming and open yourself up to new ideas and new people who support you. This involves starting with yourself and doing the inner work necessary to create a more supportive tribe. Many people are between two worlds here. They know that their old life doesn't work, but they haven't quite established the new one yet.

Recall the research of Dr. Mario Martinez, who has documented the ways in which all tribes wound the members who step beyond the pale: betrayal, abandonment, and shaming. Ask yourself if you are able to be all of who you really are within your original family and tribe. If not, there has never been a time in history that is more conducive to finding your true Soul family—despite the Soul lessons that you have inevitably had to work out along the way.

Relationship coach Diana Kirschner, who wrote *Love in 90 Days*, points out that we live in an era of abundant love. More people are finding love at all ages than ever before because of online dating and social media. The same is true for finding your Soul tribe. A word of caution, though—do not make the mistake of creating a tribe solely from a shared wound, such as incest, the loss of a child, cancer, or any other disease. Though support groups can be enormously helpful at first, too often the wound becomes the only reason for the existence of the group. And if you evolve to the point where you want to bring more joy and light into the group, you may find yourself shunned yet again.

Years ago, when I was reinventing myself after my divorce, I believed that my "real tribe"—my peers, who believed in the kinds of things that are in this book—were somewhere else. Anywhere but where I was. Certainly not in my town. Or even in my state.

I felt profoundly alone for a while there, so I set out to find my true tribe. This meant I had to step off my pedestal as a "medical authority," because intrinsic to this identity is the tendency to keep others at bay by having all the answers. I wouldn't be open to receiving what others had to give. I wanted real friends, not just people who called when they had a problem or wanted advice.

Right about this time, I began to realize that there were dozens of people just like me who were looking for good gigs, things like parties that involved real fun, not just drinking. Gatherings where we could do ceremonies on special earth days like the solstices and equinoxes—and the new moon and full moon. Ceremonies that have been done since the beginning of time to honor the cycles of the earth and the profound way in which the stars affect us. Gatherings in which we could cry or laugh at movies together while sitting on the couch and exchanging foot rubs. And maybe even spending the day watching a few movies in a row. Or hiking in the fresh air for as long as it was pleasurable.

Over time, as I allowed the walls around my heart to melt, more members of my real tribe showed up. Remarkably, a lot of them had been here all along. I just couldn't see or appreciate them until I was a vibrational match to them. I had to take off the professional armor that was protecting my heart and learn how to dance in close embrace. Which I did. Literally. From learning Argentine tango. Our tango community felt like a miracle back then—and it still does. Where else do people from all walks of life and all age groups gather together, embrace, and allow themselves the pleasure and intimacy of moving to romantic music?

In addition to my hometown tribe, I have also discovered members of my tribe in Turkey, England, Scotland, the Netherlands, Norway, Denmark, Australia, New Zealand, Germany, Spain, France, Italy, Argentina, Croatia, Mexico, Costa Rica, India, Thailand, Taiwan, China, Africa, and the Middle East. And pretty much everywhere else on the planet. The more I release my old tribal programming about what I'm "supposed" to do, say, and think in order to "fit in" to a way of being that has never matched the real me, the more my true tribe has assembled. With these people, the more I speak my truth—with a wide-open heart full of love and acceptance for myself as well as others—the more I am embraced.

Finding your Soul family is a process, but it's so worth it in the end. The way to find your people is to start by asking yourself the following: "What am I interested in? What have I always wanted to know more about? Or to see and experience? What have I always wanted to try?" And then let this truth be your guide: That which you are seeking is also seeking you.

This next step is the hard part. You must have the courage to step out on your own. Almost all of us remember those times in middle school when we were in the cafeteria with our lunch trays looking for a place to sit. And we've all had times when we ended up sitting alone. Even as adults. You can get stuck here if you aren't willing to try anything new on your own. Now here's the problem with that: Most of the people in your current tribe are not the ones in the new tribe you are seeking. So you may find yourself having to beg a friend to go with you when they don't really want to. If you're afraid to do something on your own, it's easy to dismiss the activity you have your heart set on because you don't know anyone in the new group. But resist this urge.

Practicing Stepping Out

Do you remember the practice we did in Chapter 7, where we imagined approaching someone in a coffee shop? That exercise was in essence practice for meeting people. The same thing can help us when we're afraid to go out and meet our new tribe.

Try this: Imagine yourself taking part in a new activity that you're excited about. Then imagine yourself walking up to someone who's there. Smile and say hi. Practice breaking the ice like this until it's easy. As you're doing this, remember that almost everyone feels vulnerable when it comes to meeting new people. So try to feel confident in your imagined scenario. Practice making the first move—even if that move is simply telling someone you like their outfit.

> Once you've practiced this a bit, take yourself out into the real world. Choose an event, and then walk up to someone and introduce yourself. You'll be amazed at how fast you can make new friends in social settings if you're willing to just smile and say hello. It's that simple.

Note that a good gig for finding like-minded people always has a focus—reading a book, learning a dance, traveling somewhere together, seeing a play or a movie. Are you interested in fitness? You'll find many groups at the local YMCA or gym. Yoga classes are another great place to meet people. Or if you like the outdoors, you can gather with others who like nature and being outside. Outdoor trails and beaches always need maintenance. In our area, neighbors often get together for a beach clean-up day, or a trail-maintenance day. It's a fun way to meet people and do good work at the same time.

Also keep in mind that the Internet has given us endless ways to meet people. Facebook groups are a wonderful way to find your tribe. In my Ageless Goddess Facebook group, for example, which is comprised of women who have taken my Ageless Goddess online course, many members reach out to one another via private message. They also meet up in person for coffee or other activities. They know they're already in alignment because they've been drawn to the course and the ongoing support of the group. It warms my heart to see women finding their true tribes in this way.

Whether it's a book club, an adult-education class, or a cooking class, the thing that matters is to make sure you are interacting with people who are aligned with your Soul. As long as the subject matter is something you are passionate about, there's a chance that you'll find a member of your intimate tribe at one of these gatherings.

You can belong to a number of tribes. You don't have to pick just one. But over time, you're likely to find that there will be a core group of friends and family with whom you feel most at home.

Your most intimate tribe will consist of the people you could call on in an emergency or when you really need help: the "middle of the night" tribe. Make a list of those people now. Over time you'll likely find that people are added to this list. And some will be subtracted.

Finding a group of people who truly speak to your Soul only happens when you embrace the truth of who you really are. Begin right where you are. No matter where that is.

I've been storing up the kind of knowledge presented in this book for lifetimes. But I haven't dared to speak it or write it fully—until now. Because it's time. We are at a turning point in which the old ways no longer work. Divine information is flooding in. We are surrounded by scores of angels just waiting to be asked to help. But nothing will change until we do. There's an old saying, "God moves mountains. Bring a shovel."

It is time for your life to work and to be easy. And it can be. Better than you ever dreamed possible. But you have to make the first move. Blessed be.

AFTERWORD

Now you know how to make life easy. But don't take my word for it. Go out and discover the truth of what you've learned for yourself. There's really no other way. No matter what I tell you—or what anyone else tells you—you have to put this information into practice in your own life to really understand how powerful it is.

As you start to use the techniques in this book, your biggest enemy will be fear. What if things don't work out? What if he leaves me? What if I try this new thing and it fails? What if I'm disappointed? These are the kinds of thoughts that make life hard. Always. And that's okay. In fact, being okay with fear, or grief, or disappointment is the first step on the journey to making life easy. So when fear shows up, just accept it and say, "That's okay."

The thing you need to remember about fear is that it too is part of the Divine plan. But it's kind of like the Divine in the lowest possible vibration. Matt Kahn points out that what we call "the shadow" is the light of Divinity in its most repressed form, which is inevitably uncomfortable and inconvenient. And it's like this by design. The goal of your shadow and your fear is to get you back into alignment with the more expanded form of the Divine, where life becomes easy.

Feeling fear just means that you don't yet trust that the Divine is the most powerful Source for love and delight in your life. You don't trust that everything that happens to you is beneficial— despite appearances to the contrary. You just have to learn how to trust this truth.

So what does it take to unpack that repressed Divinity and expand it so that life becomes easy? Tuning in to your emotions.

Loving yourself and that little kid inside without judgment—no matter what he or she is feeling and no matter what's happening. And also knowing that the Divine can do far more for you than you could ever figure out for yourself. But you have to partner with it.

Our emotions ground our transcendent eternal Self into our physical body. They bridge our Spirits and the material world. Imagine that. The very feelings you've been told to control or been shamed for hold the key to making life easy. Once you feel okay with anything that might not seem okay, your vibration rises and more of your Divine self downloads into your body. The result is that you become healthier and more loving, tolerant, and joyful.

Every emotion you experience is feedback from your eternal Self reminding you what needs to be done to make your life easier. We all want to feel better. We all want more joy, love, and delight in our lives. And we can all have that. Instead of following the well-worn path of despair so many of us were handed at birth, we need to choose a better way. We have to have enough faith to step into the unknown.

Now here's the really good news. This is a very special time on planet Earth. The powerful energy of Divine Love has now magnified and stabilized to such an extent that each of us can tap into this Source energy at will. This is as simple as saying "I accept Divine Love," then drawing a deep breath in through your nose, holding it for a count of four, and then pulsing it out through your nose. It's pretty easy; you just have to do it like you mean it. Divine Love will do the rest.

When you're connected to the Divine, you can feel it. And the more you feel it, the easier it becomes. You create a pathway for the Divine to make your life easy.

So just remember. Connect daily—in fact, connect every 10 to 15 minutes. Ask the Creator for guidance and help. Regularly let your Divine self lead your life. Surrender to this Source. Have the courage to make life easy and be part of the solution to the suffering of the world. Including your own. You have the power to do this. You were born for it. And I honor that about you. Blessed be.

RESOURCES

Angels and Spiritual Beings

- *Angel Blessings: Cards of Sacred Guidance and Inspiration*, by Kimberly Marooney
- Doreen Virtue, www.doreenvirtue.com
  - *Angels 101: An Introduction to Connecting, Working, and Healing with the Angels*
  - *How to Hear Your Angels*
  - *Signs from Above: Your Angels' Messages about Your Life Purpose, Relationships, Health, and More*
- Kyle Gray, www.kylegray.co.uk
  - *Angel Prayers: Harnessing the Help of Heaven to Create Miracles*
  - *Wings of Forgiveness: Working with the Angels to Release, Heal and Transform*
- *Lessons from the 12 Archangels: Divine Intervention in Daily Life*, by Belinda J. Womack
- *Natives of Eternity: An Authentic Record of Experiences in Realms of Super-Physical Consciousness*, by Flower A. Newhouse

Astrology

- Anne Ortelee: www.anneortelee.com and her weekly weather on www.blogtalkradio.com
- *Astrology, A Cosmic Science: The Classic Work on Spiritual Astrology*, by Isabel M. Hickey
- *Pronoia Is the Antidote to Paranoia: How the Whole World Is Conspiring to Shower You with Blessings*, by Rob Brezsny
- *The Only Astrology Book You'll Ever Need*, by Joanna Martine Woolfolk
- The Shamanic Astrology Mystery School (www.shamanicastrology.com)
  - *The Shamanic Astrology Handbook,* by Daniel Giamario and Cayelin Castell

Brain-Body Connection/Neuroplasticity

- *Anatomy of an Illness as Perceived by the Patient: Reflections on Healing and Regeneration*, by Norman Cousins
- Bruce H. Lipton, Ph.D., www.brucelipton.com
  - *The Biology of Belief: Unleashing the Power of Consciousness, Matter & Miracles*
  - *The Honeymoon Effect: The Science of Creating Heaven on Earth*
  - *The Wisdom of Your Cells: How Your Beliefs Control Your Biology*
- Dr. Joe Dispenza, www.drjoedispenza.com
  - *Breaking the Habit of Being Yourself: How to Lose Your Mind and Create a New One*
  - *Our Three Brains: From Thinking to Doing to Being*, TEDx, Tacoma, WA: www.drjoedispenza.com/index.php?page_id=Our_Three_Brains

- o *You Are the Placebo: Making Your Mind Matter*
- Dr. Mario Martinez, www.biocognitive.com
  - o *The MindBody Code: How to Change the Beliefs that Limit Your Health, Longevity, and Success*

Dream Interpretation

- Doris E. Cohen, Ph.D., www.drdorisecohen.com
  - o Doris does individual sessions focusing on dream interpretation and how to use their messages in daily life. She has a very specific dream guide whose insight is astounding.
- *Memories, Dreams, and Reflections*, by C. G. Jung
- *The Toltec Secret: Dreaming Practices of the Ancient Mexicans*, by Sergio Magaña
- *The Undiscovered Self: With Symbols and the Interpretation of Dreams*, by C. G. Jung

Fear and Empowerment

- *Big Magic: Creative Living Beyond Fear*, by Elizabeth Gilbert
- Brené Brown, www.brenebrown.com
  - o *Daring Greatly: How the Courage to Be Vulnerable Transforms the Way We Live, Love, Parent, and Lead*
  - o *The Gifts of Imperfection: Let Go of Who You Think You're Supposed to Be and Embrace Who You Are*
- *Empowerment: The Art of Creating Your Life as You Want It*, by David Gershon and Gail Straub

Fascia Stretching and Release

- Clear Passage, www.clearpassage.com, specializing in fascial release for surgical adhesions, bowel obstruction, and infertility
- John F. Barnes's Myofascial Release Approach, www.myofascialrelease.com
- The Genius of Flexibility, www.thegeniusofflexibility.com
- www.BendableBody.com
- *The Genius of Flexibility: The Smart Way to Stretch and Strengthen Your Body,* by Bob Cooley
- Sparhawk Pilates and the Center for Intuitive Movement Healing, www.sparhawkpilates.com

Food/Eating

- *Always Hungry?: Conquer Cravings, Retrain Your Fat Cells, and Lose Weight Permanently,* by David Ludwig
- Anthony William, www.medicalmedium.com
    - *Medical Medium: Secrets Behind Chronic and Mystery Illness and How to Finally Heal*
    - *Medical Medium Life-Changing Foods: Save Yourself and the Ones You Love with the Hidden Healing Power of Fruits & Vegetables*
- *Comparative Guide to Nutritional Supplements: A Compendium of Over 500 Products Available in the United States & Canada,* by Lyle MacWilliam
- Dr. David Perlmutter, www.drperlmutter.com
    - *Brain Maker: The Power of Gut Microbes to Heal and Protect Your Brain—for Life*

- o *Grain Brain: The Surprising Truth about Wheat, Carbs, and Sugar—Your Brain's Silent Killers*

- o *The Grain Brain Cookbook: More Than 150 Life-Changing Gluten-Free Recipes to Transform Your Health*

- Donna Schwenk, www.culturedfoodlife.com

  - o *Cultured Food for Health: A Guide to Healing Yourself with Probiotic Foods*

  - o *Cultured Food for Life: How to Make and Serve Delicious Probiotic Foods for Better Health and Wellness*

- Environmental Working Group, www.ewg.org

  - o "Dirty Dozen" and "Clean 15" lists: www.ewg.org/foodnews

- Kris Carr, www.kriscarr.com

  - o *Crazy Sexy Diet: Eat Your Veggies, Ignite Your Spark, and Live Like You Mean It!*

  - o *Crazy Sexy Juice: 100+ Simple Juice, Smoothie & Nut Milk Recipes to Supercharge Your Health*

  - o *Crazy Sexy Kitchen: 150 Plant-Empowered Recipes to Ignite a Mouthwatering Revolution*

- Dr. Mark Hyman, www.drhyman.com

  - o *The Blood Sugar Solution: The UltraHealthy Program for Losing Weight, Preventing Disease, and Feeling Great Now!*

  - o *The Blood Sugar Solution 10-Day Detox Diet: Activate Your Body's Natural Ability to Burn Fat and Lose Weight Fast*

- *The PlantPlus Diet Solution: Personalized Nutrition for Life*, by Joan Borysenko

- Thrive market, www.thrivemarket.com, delivers deeply discounted organic packaged food right to your door
- *Wheat Belly: Lose the Wheat, Lose the Weight, and Find Your Path Back to Health*, by William Davis, M.D.

Giving and Receiving

- *Living a Beautiful Life: 500 Ways to Add Elegance, Order, Beauty and Joy to Every Day of Your Life*, by Alexandra Stoddard
- *The Power of Receiving: A Revolutionary Approach to Giving Yourself the Live You Want and Deserve*, by Amanda Owen

Manifestation/Affirmations

- Abraham-Hicks, www.abraham-hicks.com
  - *Ask and It Is Given: Learning to Manifest Your Desires*, by Esther and Jerry Hicks
  - *The Law of Attraction: The Basic Teachings of Abraham*, by Esther and Jerry Hicks
- Daily affirmations delivered to your in-box from my website, www.drnorthrup.com
- Louise Hay, www.louisehay.com
  - *Heal Your Body*
  - *Meditations to Heal Your Life*
  - *Mirror Work: 21 Days to Heal Your Life*
  - *You Can Heal Your Life*
- *The Dynamic Laws of Prosperity*, by Catherine Ponder

- *The Magic Path of Intuition*, by Florence Scovel Shinn
- *Think and Grow Rich*, by Napoleon Hill

Medicine/Physical Health

- Amata Life, www.amatalife.com
  - Hormone balance for women and men. Because of the astounding benefits of the herb *Pueraria mirifica* from Thailand, Dr. Northrup started a company to bring these products to the attention of people worldwide. Her product line, Amata Life, contains a patented extract of *Pueraria mirifica* and works beautifully for menstrual symptoms, perimenopausal symptoms, and menopausal symptoms in women and also helps protect male prostate health. The skin care and vaginal moisturizer line have helped hundreds.
- Anthony William, www.medicalmedium.com
  - *Medical Medium: Secrets Behind Chronic and Mystery Illness and How to Finally Heal*
  - *Medical Medium Life-Changing Foods: Save Yourself and the Ones You Love with the Hidden Healing Power of Fruits & Vegetables*
- Christiane Northrup, M.D., www.drnorthrup.com
  - *Goddesses Never Age: The Secret Prescription for Radiance, Vitality, and Well-Being*
  - *Women's Bodies, Women's Wisdom: Creating Physical and Emotional Health and Healing*
  - *Mother-Daughter Wisdom: Understanding the Crucial Link Between Mothers, Daughters, and Health*
  - *The Wisdom of Menopause: Creating Physical and Emotional Health During the Change*

- *Counterclockwise: Mindful Health and the Power of Possibility*, by Dr. Ellen J. Langer

- Edgar Cayce's Association for Research and Enlightenment, www.edgarcayce.org

- *Health Revelations from Heaven and Earth*, by Tommy Rosa and Stephen Sinatra

- Katy Bowman, Nutritious Movement, www.nutritiousmovement.com

  o *Katy Says* podcast

  o *Move Your DNA: Restore Your Health Through Natural Movement*

  o *Whole Body Barefoot: Transitioning Well to Minimal Footwear*

- *Let Magic Happen: Adventures in Healing with a Holistic Radiologist*, by Larry Burk, M.D.

- *Love, Medicine & Miracles: Lessons Learned about Self-Healing from a Surgeon's Experience with Exceptional Patients*, by Dr. Bernie S. Siegel

- *Radical Remission: The Nine Key Factors That Can Make a Real Difference*, by Dr. Kelly A. Turner

- *Sitting Kills, Moving Heals: How Everyday Movement Will Prevent Pain, Illness, and Early Death—and Exercise Alone Won't*, by Joan Vernikos, Ph.D.

- Sparhawk Pilates and Center for Intuitive Movement Healing with Hope Matthews, www.sparhawkpilates.com

- *The Relaxation Response*, by Herbert Benson, M.D.

- The Tapping Solution, www.thetappingsolution.com

  o *The Tapping Solution: A Revolutionary System for Stress-Free Living*, by Nick Ortner

  o *The Tapping Solution* documentary film

- o *The Tapping Solution for Weight Loss & Body Confidence: A Woman's Guide to Stressing Less, Weighing Less, and Loving More,* by Jessica Ortner
- Yoga Toes, www.yogapro.com/products/YogaToes.html

Narcissism and Narcissistic Abuse

- Melanie Tonia Evans, www.melanietoniaevans.com
- Sandra Brown, Institute for Relational Harm Reduction and Public Pathology Education, www.womenwholovepsychopaths.com
  - o *How to Spot a Dangerous Man before You Get Involved*
  - o *Women Who Love Psychopaths: Inside the Relationships of Inevitable Harm with Psychopaths, Sociopaths & Narcissists*
- Understanding and Healing for Daughters of Narcissistic Mothers, www.daughtersof narcissisticmothers/narcissistic-personality-disorder/

Oracle/Tarot Card Reading

- *Angel Prayer Oracle Cards,* by Kyle Gray
- *Goddess Guidance Oracle Cards,* by Doreen Virtue
- *Medicine Cards: The Discovery of Power Through the Ways of Animals,* by Jamie Sams and David Carson
- Motherpeace Round Tarot Deck, by Karen Vogel and Vicki Noble
- *Uncharted: The Journey through Uncertainty to Infinite Possibility,* by Colette Baron-Reid

- *Wisdom of the Oracle Divination Cards: Ask and Know,* by Colette Baron-Reid

Prayer/Connection with the Divine

- *Angel Prayers: Harnessing the Help of Heaven to Create Miracles,* by Kyle Gray
- *Healing Words: The Power of Prayer and the Practice of Medicine,* by Larry Dossey, M.D.
- *Help, Thanks, Wow: The Three Essential Prayers,* by Anne Lamott
- Proprioceptive Writing with Linda Trichter Metcalf, www.radix00.com/PWriting_Main
- Robert Fritchie, World Service Institute and the Divine Love healing process, www.worldserviceinstitute.org
  - o *Being at One with the Divine: Self-Healing with Divine Love*
  - o *Divine Love Self Healing: The At Oneness Healing System*
  - o Divine Love Healing Process webinar (free): www.worldserviceinstitute.org/fhp-program.html
- Tosha Silver, www.toshasilver.com
  - o *Change Me Prayers: The Hidden Power of Spiritual Surrender*
  - o *Outrageous Openness: Letting the Divine Take the Lead*
  - o Tosha also leads a group called the Forum, which includes weekly calls from her and a private Facebook group for members.

Reincarnation/Past Lives

- Brian Weiss, www.brianweiss.com

  o *Many Lives, Many Masters: The True Story of a Prominent Psychiatrist, His Young Patient, and the Past-Life Therapy That Changed Both Their Lives*

  o *Same Soul, Many Bodies: Discover the Healing Power of Future Lives Through Progression Therapy*

- Denise Linn, www.deniselinn.com

  o Denise does past-life regressions, dream work, space clearing, and many other types of healing.

  o *Past Lives, Present Miracles: The Most Empowering Book on Reincarnation You'll Ever Read . . . in This Lifetime!*

- Doris E. Cohen, Ph.D., www.drdorisecohen.com

  o Dr. Cohen does individual past-life regressions.

  o *Repetition: Past Lives, Life, and Rebirth*

- *Reincarnation & Karma*, by Edgar Cayce

- Robert Fritchie, Divine Love Self Healing: The At Oneness Healing System, www.worldserviceinstitute .org/at-oneness-healing-system.html

Sexuality and Vital Life Force

- Amata Life, www.amatalife.com

  o Hormone balance for women and men. Because of the astounding benefits of the herb *Pueraria mirifica* from Thailand, Dr. Northrup started a company to bring these products to the attention of people worldwide. Her product line, Amata Life, contains a patented extract of *Pueraria mirifica* and works beautifully for menstrual symptoms, perimenopausal symptoms, and menopausal symptoms in women and also helps protect male prostate health. The skin care and vaginal moisturizer line have helped hundreds.

- *Getting to "I Do": The Secret to Doing Relationships Right,* by Dr. Patricia Allen and Sandra Harmon

- *The Illustrated Guide to Extended Massive Orgasm,* by Drs. Steve and Vera Bodansky

- *Love in 90 Days: The Essential Guide to Finding Your Own True Love,* by Diana Kirschner, Ph.D.

- *Money, A Love Story: Untangle Your Financial Woes and Create the Life You Really Want,* by Kate Northrup

- *The Multi-Orgasmic Man: Sexual Secrets Every Man Should Know,* by Mantak Chia and Douglas Abrams

- *Orgasm Matters,* by Steve Bodansky

- Regena Thomashauer, Mama Gena's School of Womanly Arts, www.mamagenas.com

  o *Mama Gena's School of Womanly Arts: Using the Power of Pleasure to Have Your Way with the World*

  o *Pussy: A Reclamation*

- *Sacred Success: A Course in Financial Miracles,* by Barbara Stanny

- *Succulent SexCraft: Your Hands-On Guide to Erotic Play and Practice,* by Sheri Winston with Carl Frankel

- *Tao Tantric Arts for Women: Cultivating Sexual Energy, Love, and Spirit,* by Minke de Vos

- *Think and Grow Rich,* by Napoleon Hill

- *Women's Anatomy of Arousal: Secret Maps to Buried Pleasure,* by Sheri Winston

- *Worthy: Boost Your Self-Worth to Grow Your Net Worth,* by Nancy Levin

- *Vagina*, by Naomi Wolf
- Yoni egg sources: www.jadeeggs.com and www.etsy.com

Soul/Spirit/Ego and the Collective Unconscious

- *Ask and It Is Given: Learning to Manifest Your Desires*, by Esther and Jerry Hicks
- *The Ego and the Id*, by Sigmund Freud
- *Dancing in the Flames: The Dark Goddess in the Transformation of Consciousness*, by Marion Woodman and Elinor Dickson
- *The Game of Life and How to Play It*, by Florence Scovel Shinn
- *Help, Thanks, Wow: The Three Essential Prayers*, by Anne Lamott
- Matt Kahn, www.truedivinenature.com
  - o *Whatever Arises, Love That: A Love Revolution That Begins with You*
- *Meet Your Soul: A Powerful Guide to Connect with Your Most Sacred Self*, by Elisa Romeo
- *Modern Man in Search of a Soul*, by C. G. Jung
- *Not for Sale: Finding Center in the Land of Crazy Horse*, by Kevin Hancock
- *One Mind: How Our Individual Mind Is Part of a Greater Consciousness and Why It Matters*, by Larry Dossey, M.D.
- *Traveling Mercies: Some Thoughts on Faith*, by Anne Lamott

Spiritual/Energetic Healing

- *Original Blessing: A Primer in Creation Spirituality Presented in Four Paths, Twenty-Six Themes, and Two Questions*, by Matthew Fox

- The Global Coherence Initiative, www.heartmath.com/gci

- Melanie Ericksen, Soul Play with Melanie, www.soulplay.us

- Peter Calhoun

  o *Last Hope on Earth: A Revolutionary Approach to Healing and Wellness that Can Transform Your Life* (with Astrid Ganz)

  o *Soul on Fire: A Transformational Journey from Priest to Shaman*

- The Realization Process created by Judith Blackstone, www.realizationcenter.com

- Robert Fritchie, World Service Institute and the Divine Love healing process, www .worldserviceinstitute.org

  o *Being at One with the Divine: Self-Healing with Divine Love*

  o *Divine Love Self Healing: The At Oneness Healing System*

  o Divine Love Healing Process webinar (free): www .worldserviceinstitute.org/fhp-program.html

- Sparhawk Pilates and the Center for Intuitive Movement Healing, www.sparhawkpilates.com

INDEX

Kirschner, Diana, 211
Kübler-Ross, Elisabeth, 208
Kundalini, 178, 179

L

Lamott, Anne, 102
Langer, Ellen, 135
Let Magic Happen (Burk), 48
Levy, Noah, 124
License plates, 52
Life force. *See* Vital life force
Life that works, 3–4, 6
Lipton, Bruce, 7
Living a Beautiful Life (Stoddard), 81
Loss, 11, 108
Love, Medicine & Miracles (Siegel), 123
Love in 90 Days (Kirschner), 211
Ludwig, David, 154, 161
Ludwig, Dawn, 161

M

Magaña, Sergio, 47–48
Magical thinking, 47
Magnesium, 171
Maharishi Mahesh Yogi, 75
Mama Gena's School of Womanly Arts, 183
Manifestation, 94
Marketing, 210–11
Marooney, Kimberly, 178–79
Martinez, Mario, 7, 31, 81, 112, 124, 128, 135–36, 172, 211
Masculine energies, 59–61
Mass media, 66
Masturbation, 192
Matter, 9, 11
Matthews, Hope, 145
Mayo Clinic, 4

McGarey, Gladys, 10–11
Meaning, searching for, 115–17
Medical Medium (William), 43, 154, 160
Medical school, xi–xii, 2
Medicine, Western, xii, 4
  fear and, 97
Medicine Cards (Sams), 50, 54
Meditation, 74–76, 77, 183
  breathing, 75
  Realization Process, 75–76
Meeting people, practicing, 100, 213–14
Messages from the universe, 45–62
  dreams, 47–51
  oracle cards, 53–54
  psychics, 53–54, 57
  signs and symbols, 45–47, 50, 52–53
  songs, 38, 51–52
  synchronicities, 58–61
  tarot cards, 53–57
Metcalf, Linda Trichter, 71, 72
Microbiome, 167–68, 204
Microcosmic orbit exercise, 191–92, 194
Mind, 63. *See also* Thoughts
  as builder, 6–7
  health and, 6–7
  unity of body, Spirit, and, 4–5
MindBody Code, The (Martinez), 7, 112
Money, 69–71, 107
Monogamy, 187–88
Moody, Raymond, 16
Morphic field, 14, 93
  of the past, clearing, 15–16
Mount Shasta, 59–60, 61
Movement, 139, 141–44
Movies, 48–49
Mozart effect, 73
MSG (monosodium glutamate), 155–56, 157

ACKNOWLEDGMENTS

This has been the easiest book I've ever written. Because I now know and practice the message contained in these pages. Making life easy requires being wide open to receiving assistance and guidance. The following individuals have provided that in spades—and I am so humbly grateful.

Laura Gray, my editorial assistant—you have that New York edge and Midwestern groundedness, all wrapped into one. Thank you so much for being the midwife for this book and for making my words sound so much better.

Anne Barthel, my editor at Hay House—what a pleasure to work with you again, and to have the editorial process be so easy to implement. Just thrilling to me.

Patty Gift—thanks for overseeing this project from big picture to finished book. With such style and fun. As always.

Christy Salinas—your artistic eye has created another great book cover. Thank you so much for orchestrating the most fun and productive photo shoot I've ever enjoyed. And for being a visual genius.

Reid Tracy and Margarete Nielsen—having both of you at the helm of Hay House combines the best of business and family. I love working with such visionary, fun, skillful, and intuitive people.

Diane Ray and the entire team at Hay House Radio—I just love my weekly Hay House radio show *Flourish!* and the global community of people I get to interact with regularly. I can finally teach what I've always wanted people to know.

Richelle Fredson, my Hay House publicist—you are, hands down, the most effective and delightful publicist I've ever worked with. I'll follow your lead anywhere.

The entire staff at Hay House—thank you for supporting my work on all levels with such enthusiasm and skill. I appreciate all of you.

Hope Matthews, my Pilates and Intuitive Movement healer extraordinaire—you have borne witness to and catalyzed my personal transformation for many years through your knowledge of both classical Pilates and the impact of emotions on the body. With the added Resistance Flexibility, I get to experience my body becoming stronger and more flexible with each passing year. What a gift!

Julie Hofheimer, my massage therapist and intuitive healer— you have kept my muscles and my spirit supple and tuned for many years, and you've seen and documented the rebirth of my body. Thank you.

Paulina Carr, my girl Friday—I can't tell you how grateful I am that you are willing to do whatever it takes to keep the ship of my life and business afloat. Even if it involves a truck and multiple trips to the post office. Thanks always for all that you do. And the humor with which you do it. And also the fact that you are a stylish ageless goddess.

Janet Lambert, my trusty bookkeeper—thank you for being the keeper of the finances by day. And by night. And on weekends, a true ageless goddess water-skier, scuba diver, and skydiver. You are an inspiration.

Coulson Duerksen, my online editor for www.drnorthrup.com—thank you for being a tuned-in writer and editor who has a finger on the pulse of everything that is healthy and sustainable. You're a great addition to the team. And a treasure to work with.

Tosha Silver—you arrived in my life at precisely the right moment to remind me of Divine Order and how to use it. The healing of my life and heart have been profound. And a new era has begun. For both of us. And it can all turn on a dime.

Bob Fritchie—thank you, thank you, thank you for your dedication to Divine Love and for creating a practical method for bringing this to everyone in the world. I so appreciate your being personally available to me and my family. Thank you also for being such a good friend, guide, and mentor. I appreciate you beyond words.

Doris E. Cohen—thank you for teaching me the power of dreams. And for bringing this magic into my life regularly for so many years.

Deborah Kern—Thank you for your friendship, your mirroring, your Divine presence, your moon in Pisces, your transformation. All of it.

Melanie Ericksen, the fabulous Mermaid Medicine Woman—I feel so much gratitude for the new moon and full moon ceremonies that keep us so delightfully connected with Mother Earth, our lunar natures, and the joys of friendship.

Priscilla Reynolds—thank you for being my soul sister despite years of separation. Our paths and stories delight me beyond words. And the best is yet to come.

All the skilled and loyal members of my "assisted living" program here at home—thank you. Stephen Meehan, who has, quite literally, created heaven on earth right here in my yard with his in-depth knowledge of plants, flowers, and beauty. This brings me so much joy and pleasure. Mike Meehan and crew for the plowing and shoveling and tree work, cheerfully accomplished at 5 A.M. Mike Brewer for being a most reliable and cheerful handyman for many years. Carlo Dorio for rescuing me from any and all plumbing emergencies and being a delight to work with. Vern and Mike Cassidy, my father/son electrical geniuses, for maintaining all the things that keep it "lit up" around here. Charlie Grover for being such a steadfast, twinkle-in-the-eye presence for decades, supporting my life and business with such humility and humor. And Pat McCabe for housekeeping skill and charm—and for loving Mr. Moon.

My brothers and my incredible sisters-in-law, John and Annie, Bill and Lori—your support, love, and friendship grow ever more precious to me. John, I treasure your business and financial know-how and support. We must have done something right in a past life to show up now and enjoy each other so much.

My sister, Penny, and her husband, Phil (who calls us his sister-wives)—thank you so much for the cappuccinos, the Budwig breakfasts, the workouts, the beach walks. And the Team Northrup partnership and vision. The inspiration, friendship, and laughs that you both provide, not just for me but for hundreds of others.

Mom—thank you for the backbone and the discipline. And for remaining an ageless role model for so many. May you find your life increasingly easy and joyful.

Annie and Katie, my beautiful daughters—you are jewels in my life. You make it sing with beauty and joy. And meaning. Thank you for choosing me to be your mother.

Penelope Ann, my granddaughter—I am entranced with you. And at the prospect of all our adventures together. Starting with fairy houses. And thanks to your father, Mike, for being such a good dad.

And finally, Diane Grover, my CEO of Everything—the woman behind the woman. You have mothered me, comforted me, stood by me as I have learned how to make life easy. You have stuck by me even when I wasn't making anything easy. With love and support. You are a steadfast and joyful presence in my life. You make it all worthwhile. And fun. You are the pearl of great price. Don't even think of retiring.

ABOUT THE AUTHOR

Christiane Northrup, M.D., board-certified ob/gyn, former assistant clinical professor of ob/gyn at the University of Vermont College of Medicine, *New York Times* best-selling author, is a visionary pioneer in women's health. After decades on the front lines of her profession as a practicing physician in obstetrics and gynecology, she is now dedicating her life to helping women truly flourish by learning how to enhance all that can go *right* with their bodies. Dr. Northrup is a leading proponent of medicine that acknowledges the unity of mind, body, emotions, and spirit. Internationally known for her empowering approach to women's health and wellness, she teaches women (and many men) how to thrive at every stage of life and encourages them to create health on all levels by tuning in to their inner wisdom.

As a business owner, physician, former surgeon, mother, writer, and speaker, Dr. Northrup acknowledges our individual and collective capacity for growth, freedom, joy, and balance. She is also thrilled with her company Amata, whose name is derived from the Thai words for "ageless" and "eternal." This company is devoted to creating and distributing products that contribute to vibrant health and well-being throughout the life cycle (www.amatalife.com).

When she's not traveling, Dr. Northrup loves devoting her leisure time to dancing Argentine tango, staying fit through Pilates and resistance stretching, going to the movies, getting together with friends and family, potluck dinners, boating, process painting, and reading.

Dr. Northrup stays in touch with her worldwide community through her Internet radio show *Flourish!*, Facebook, Twitter, Instagram, her e-letter, and her website, www.drnorthrup.com.

Hay House Titles of Related Interest

YOU CAN HEAL YOUR LIFE, the movie, starring Louise Hay & Friends
(available as a 1-DVD program and an expanded 2-DVD set)
Watch the trailer at: www.LouiseHayMovie.com

THE SHIFT, the movie, starring Dr. Wayne W. Dyer
(available as a 1-DVD program and an expanded 2-DVD set)
Watch the trailer at: www.DyerMovie.com

***

*DYING TO BE ME: My Journey from Cancer, to Near Death,
to True Healing,* by Anita Moorjani

LIFE'S OPERATING MANUAL: With the Fear and Truth Dialogues,
by Tom Shadyac

PUSSY: A Reclamation, by Regena Thomashauer

RESILIENCE FROM THE HEART: The Power to Thrive in Life's Extremes,
by Gregg Braden

YOU CAN HEAL YOUR LIFE, by Louise Hay

All of the above are available at your local bookstore,
or may be ordered by contacting Hay House (see next page).

***

We hope you enjoyed this Hay House book. If you'd like to receive our online catalog featuring additional information on Hay House books and products, or if you'd like to find out more about the Hay Foundation, please contact:

Hay House, Inc., P.O. Box 5100, Carlsbad, CA 92018-5100
(760) 431-7695 or (800) 654-5126
(760) 431-6948 (fax) or (800) 650-5115 (fax)
www.hayhouse.com® • www.hayfoundation.org

* * *

Published and distributed in Australia by: Hay House Australia Pty. Ltd.,
18/36 Ralph St., Alexandria NSW 2015
Phone: 612-9669-4299 • *Fax:* 612-9669-4144 • www.hayhouse.com.au

Published and distributed in the United Kingdom by: Hay House UK, Ltd.,
Astley House, 33 Notting Hill Gate, London W11 3JQ
Phone: 44-20-3675-2450 • *Fax:* 44-20-3675-2451 • www.hayhouse.co.uk

Published and distributed in the Republic of South Africa by:
Hay House SA (Pty), Ltd., P.O. Box 990, Witkoppen 2068
info@hayhouse.co.za • www.hayhouse.co.za

Published in India by: Hay House Publishers India,
Muskaan Complex, Plot No. 3, B-2, Vasant Kunj, New Delhi 110 070
Phone: 91-11-4176-1620 • *Fax:* 91-11-4176-1630 • www.hayhouse.co.in

Distributed in Canada by: Raincoast Books,
2440 Viking Way, Richmond, B.C. V6V 1N2
Phone: 1-800-663-5714 • *Fax:* 1-800-565-3770 • www.raincoast.com

* * *

<u>**Take Your Soul on a Vacation**</u>

Visit www.HealYourLife.com® to regroup, recharge,
and reconnect with your own magnificence.
Featuring blogs, mind-body-spirit news, and life-changing
wisdom from Louise Hay and friends.

Visit www.HealYourLife.com today!

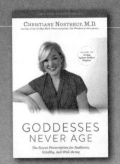

Free e-newsletters
from Hay House, the Ultimate
Resource for Inspiration

Be the first to know about Hay House's dollar deals, free downloads, special offers, affirmation cards, giveaways, contests, and more!

 Get exclusive excerpts from our latest releases and videos from *Hay House Present Moments*.

 Enjoy uplifting personal stories, how-to articles, and healing advice, along with videos and empowering quotes, within *Heal Your Life*.

 Have an inspirational story to tell and a passion for writing? Sharpen your writing skills with insider tips from *Your Writing Life*.

Sign Up Now!

Get inspired, educate yourself, get a complimentary gift, and share the wisdom!

http://www.hayhouse.com/newsletters.php

Visit www.hayhouse.com to sign up today!

 HAY HOUSE

 HAYHOUSE RADIO
radio for your soul

HealYourLife.com ♥